Playboys of the Western World

Production Histories

Playboys of the Western World
Production Histories

Edited by Adrian Frazier

Carysfort Press

A Carysfort Press Book

Playboys of the Western World: Production Histories

First published in Ireland in 2004 as a paperback original by Carysfort Press, 58 Woodfield, Scholarstown Road, Dublin 16, Ireland

Typeset by Carysfort Press
Cover design by Alan Bennis
Printed and bound by eprint Limited
35 Coolmine Industrial Estate, Blanchardstown,
Dublin 15, Ireland

The publication of this work was supported by a grant from the NUI, Galway, and also by the Arts Council Title by Title Scheme.

the arts council
an chomhairle ealaíon

Table of Contents

PLAYBOY 2004: EIGHT VIEWS

Acknowledgements

This book arose out of an offer in December 2003 by Garry Hynes, Artistic Director of Druid, to make the theatre available for a conference on *The Playboy of the Western World* during the run of her production of that play. It was to be organized by the MA in Drama and Theatre Studies at Hynes's alma mater, the National University of Ireland, Galway. John Marshall, Dean of the Arts Faculty at the university, liked the idea and helped to fund it.

Rather than a conference on J. M. Synge and his works, textual analysis of the play, or the significance of its first performance to the Irish Literary Revival, it was decided to focus on the long production history of this Irish classic. Leading experts on Synge and Irish theatre when invited to address specific productions of *The Playboy* worked away with relish, and thanks are due to all those named in the table of contents. Lelia Doolan and Jennifer Johnston came along for the sport, but they did a lot more than that. It would be hard to find someone who is an Abbey actress, Abbey artistic director, expert broadcaster, and university teacher in broadcast journalism to moderate the roundtable discussion, but Lelia Doolan is all that, and Jennifer Johnston's wise and humorous participation in the discussion was an unexpected treat.

One contributor to the conference was unable to contribute to the book. Illness in the family did not keep Joe Donoghue from giving his talk on the day, a fascinating account from a celebrated director in the West of Ireland of why amateur companies in the area shy away from *The Playboy of the Western World.* However, an illness after the conference put Joe Donoghue briefly in hospital, so he was unable to participate in writing the book. That is a pity, because no one else knows what he knows, or could speak of it half so well.

The managing director of Druid, Fergal McGrath, did a large share of the work amiably and efficiently: organizing all the business of the conference itself, getting the proceedings taped and photographed, supplying illustrations for the text, and answering specific queries about the production itself. Thanks are also due to Francis O'Connor, set designer of the Druid 2004 *Playboy*, for answering questions from writers of this book.

An important feature of the book is its illustrative matter, mostly photographs of earlier productions of the play. Thanks are due to the photographers themselves (where known, individually credited with the illustrations): Catherine Ashmore, John Haynes, Paul McCarthy, and Keith Pattison. The book owes a lot to the work of Christopher Fitz-Simons, a director himself and author of two illustrated books on the Irish Theatre. Several images were scanned from *The Irish Theatre* (1983). There are splendid photographs, by the way, in Fitz-Simon's *The Abbey Theatre: Ireland's National Theatre: The First 100 Years*, currently for sale and available in most good bookshops.

There is practically no book that touches on the Irish Literary Revival that is not obliged to thank Colin Smythe, either for publishing the book, authorizing the use of material by George Moore, Lady Gregory, or AE, or allowing the reproduction of photographs in his collection. We must thank him for images of Maire O'Neill as Pegeen Mike.

Dan Farrelly, editor of Carysfort Press, showed interest in the project early on, and came to Galway for the conference itself. With Dan as a collaborator, the book was actually conceived prior to the conference, which itself was, as a result, a stage in the composition of the text. He worked with remarkable professionalism to bring the book together and with still more remarkable speed to bring it out. His contribution as publisher to shedding light on Irish theatre today has been a great stimulant to both scholars and practitioners alike.

Support from John Marshall, Dean, and the Arts Faculty, NUIG, made the original conference possible, and the Grant-in-Aid of Publications Fund, National University of Ireland, Galway, graciously contributed to making this book possible.

Adrian Frazier

List of Illustrations

Introduction

Adrian Frazier

Synge's *The Playboy of the Western World* is a well-studied play if there ever was one. Publishing on the subject is nearly a required rite of passage for scholars of Irish literature. But generally, they write only about the January 1907 first production and the public disturbances that attended it; the revivals over the last ninety-seven years are ignored.[1] So one purpose of this collection of essays is to give the sort of concentrated and informed attention to productions of *The Playboy of the Western World* as before has been given to its text or to its first performance alone.

Another purpose of the collection is to give to a theatrical production – in this case, Druid's 2004 *Playboy* – the prolonged, probing consideration a contemporary cultural event deserves. In the late nineteenth century, great writers like Henry James, G. B. Shaw, and Max Beerbohm wrote about the theatre for the serious London weeklies, and they were allowed three to four thousand words for an article.[2] With since unrivalled profun-

---

1 An exemplary exception is chapter three of John Harrington's *The Irish Play on the New York Stage*, which treats of the 1911 production of *The Playboy* in America (University Press of Kentucky: Lexington, 1997).

2 George Rowell, ed., *Victorian Dramatic Criticism* (Methuen: London, 1971).

dity, Soren Kierkegaard wrote ten thousand words in 1843 on the experience of attending a farce at the Königstäter Theatre, Denmark.[3] Today, it is primarily a few newspapers in each city that cover theatre events, with a few score or a few hundred words by a staff journalist. The serious weeklies and monthlies are gone. Not just the scope, but the conception of the drama review has dwindled. Reviewers now state the premise and character set, then assign adjectives to the personnel involved in its representation. Finally, the reviewer gives a verdict. Such reviews serve the public by telling them what's on, who's in it, and whether in the reviewer's judgement readers should buy tickets or give the show a miss. That's what a review now is, and that is all the newspaper editor allows it to be. No, that exaggerates the sadness of the state of theatrical affairs. But even writers as talented and passionate about the craft as Charlie McBride (*Galway Advertiser*), Karen Fricker (*Guardian*), or the team at *The Irish Times* – Fintan O'Toole, Belinda McKeon, Gerry Colgan, and Helen Meaney – can only do so much under the constraints imposed. The colour pictures, the column inches, and the enthusiastically descriptive prose have all shifted to the Property Section of the dailies.

Quite apart from whether theatre is well-served by the genre as currently conceived, reviews are a shaky basis for understanding what happened when the lights went down and the curtain went up. Action, characterization, and set are not described in detail – there's no room for such description, and judgement rather than description is the critic's contemporary brief. How the various members of the audience felt, and why, also passes unrecorded because unknown and irrelevant to the form as presently practised. Consequently, theatre historians and contemporary playgoers often make the mistake of assuming that what the reviewer said about a show is what the other spectators thought, and that what other people got from the experience boils down to whether they 'liked it' or didn't.

[3] Soren Kierkegaard, *Repetition: An Essay in Experimental Psychology* (Harper Torchbooks, Princeton University Press: Princeton, 1944), pp.60-81.

For instance, we believe we know what Dublin thought of The Playboy of the Western World in 1907: they found it offensive, and took public action to prevent its being staged. But here is an unpublished letter from Yeats about a group of people that liked what they knew of The Playboy:

> The curious thing is that I do really believe Synge has had far more sympathy from the women he is supposed to have attacked than from the men. A copy of the Play went astray by some curious chance, which I cannot trace, and it alighted, above all places in the world, in a Convent school, in the neighbourhood of Dundrum. The girls lent it to one another, and read it in a sort of terrified delight. Fifteen of them made up a plan to come to the Theatre and see the play, and come round afterwards in a deputation to thank Synge, but the nuns found a letter, expounding this plan, and so prevented it coming off. My sisters have this story from one of the girls. [4]

In addition, the Catholic anti-clerical journalist Pat Kenny, author of a book with the still attractive title *How We Drink, How We Think* (1903), defended *The Playboy* in print and public debate. [5] We also know what those January 1907 spectators thought who were arraigned for riotous behaviour, such as Padraic Colum's father and Piaras Béaslaí, or at least what they said they thought, because they gave evidence in court. Joseph Holloway's reaction is on record: in his diary he echoed the judgement that the play was slanderous on the good people of the West and the reputation of Irish women for chastity. But there is much about that audience that we do not know but simply assume.

Yeats sometimes thought that in a theatre a crowd becomes a nation, that is, a people with a sense of civic organization, customs, and a history. At other times, as in January 1907, he thought it became a mob, that is, a crowd under the temporary dominion of a single emotion. It may also be that a theatre

---

[4] WBY to John Quinn, 18 February 1907; New York Public Library.

[5] Lionel Pilkington, ' "The Most Unpopular Man in Ireland": P.D. Kenny, J. M. Synge and Irish Cultural History', *the irish review* (Autumn 2002), pp.51-57.

audience is like not just a nation or a mob, but a school of fish or chevron of geese or flock of sheep: all head in the direction in which one first turns. *The Playboy* audience, any audience perhaps, may follow like a flock a bellwether reviewer, or the first loud-mouth to cry out from the pit. They then in part believe they feel what they have been told they ought to feel. That would give crucial significance to the reviewer, or his extra-professional equivalent in the pub, more perhaps than is reasonable, but still it is possible that opinion about such events is formulated by a minority and acceded to by others.

Possible, yes, but it seems to me that the unrecorded and now unknowable responses of many spectators to a past theatre event were likely to have been as various and specific as their own individualities. Indeed, maybe it is time to reconsider Annie Horniman's letter to G. A. Bedford in the Lord Chamberlain's office, London, when as leaseholder of the Abbey Theatre, she was trying to get a license for *The Playboy* to be performed in England.[6] The Lord Chamberlain had held up the licence after the Dublin riots out of suspicion that the play was incendiary, or immoral, or obscene. In her letter, Horniman wrote that 'there was no touch of ordinary sexual immorality in Mr. Synge's work'. The opposition to the play was organized, she explained, by branches of the Gaelic League and supporters of Sinn Féin, and for several reasons: a) the protestors disapproved of Horniman's management of the theatre, because she was a patriotic Englishwoman opposed to Irish independence; b) they had romantic rather than well-informed ideas about Irish peasants on the western seaboard; c) they were opposed to an Irish dramatic tradition developing in the English rather than in the Irish language; d) they detested Yeats's position that art and not politics was the sole consideration in determining the stageworthiness of a play. After deliberation, Bedford agreed with Horniman that the outcry in Dublin was

[6] Horniman to G. A. Bedford, 17 May 1907; National Library of Ireland; see Adrian Frazier, *Behind the Scenes: Yeats, Horniman, and the Struggle for the Abbey Theatre* (University of California Press: Berkeley and Los Angeles, 1990), pp.219-221.

the result of a cabal to organize a demonstration for political purposes, and that no offence was likely to be taken to the play by audiences in England. And none was. So perhaps it was more the circumstances around the play, and less what was said and done on stage, that brought feeling to the pitch of public obstruction.Certainly, the word 'shifts' in Act Three took on an appearance of importance out of keeping with its probable significance to playgoers.

This collection of essays makes manifest the variety of response on the part of the eight writers who contributed pieces about the Druid performances in Galway in the week of 9-14 February 2004. While they have broadly similar backgrounds – a scholarly crew, and intellectual, with a long fascination with theatre or Synge or both – their responses to the show are really quite different. All the writers attended the same conference on 14 February in Druid Theatre, at which versions of the chapters printed here on the production history of *The Playboy* were delivered to an audience of about sixty. The highlight of the afternoon was a roundtable discussion with director Garry Hynes, edited and transcribed for this book. Like those authors in the late 19th century weeklies, the eight writers were then given rein for lengthy and personal essays on the 2004 Druid *Playboy*. It would be a pity to short-circuit the experiment by a featureless summary of the essays, but it can be said that from this audience sample, spectators at a show do not think alike and they often think deeply about what the play and the particular performance of it mean to them, about the world, both as it once was, and as it now is. They do not just award points or stars to the various artistes, like a panel of judges at an Olympic ice-skating trial.

It is not simply that, as Nietzsche held, to judge is to be unjust, but that the interest of a performance event in which so many talents conspire and witnesses join cannot be represented in a single verdict. The rehearsal process on a great text, if carried out by gifted actors under an intelligent director, marries the intellectual excitements of a seminar of scholars, a banquet of wits, and an artists' workshop busy with the building of a new masterpiece. A theatre event may be scuplted in snow, it passes and leaves no form behind, but for certain hours while the curtain's drawn it can be like museum statuary, yet moving.

If a theatre audience is in fact like a jury, it is not primarily the production values that they are empanelled to judge; their purpose is to come to terms morally with the events represented, as they are represented, that is, to be meaningful and provocative of social feelings. After the semiotic storm concludes, the audience leaves stunned, wondering what it is that they have felt, and how they may speak of it to their companions. It is then that a major phase of the value of theatre-going begins: the phase of discussion and reliving with friends certain passing moments or images from the show that have lodged in the memory. Reenactment among friends, debates with them, sometimes turning fierce and personal, and awakening hatred for a harmless player or defensive and sensitive love for how a character acted in an imaginary situation, are a key part of the value of a play as a cultural event. Criticism such as one finds in this book is simply a formal extension of such responsiveness.

The writers see in the 2004 Druid *Playboy* signs of the times, just as surely as historians see *The Playboy* riots as symptomatic of Dublin society in 1907. Ophelia Byrne, for instance, finds a surprising manifestation of the power of a woman even in the midst of a patriarchal society in the characterization of the Widow Quin. Mary King and Bill McCormack sense the presence of the dark history of industrial schools in the set design by Francis O'Connor. Lionel Pilkington diagnoses the Celtic Tiger embourgeoisement of Irish society in the Galway production. I suspected I was looking at an allusion to the murderous, drunken, male gang beatings of modern Dublin in the menacing hunger for blood in Act Three, perhaps simply because three boys from Blackrock College were on trial for manslaughter at the time, after kicking to death another student outside the Burlington Hotel. A work of art, Stendhal suggested, is a mirror in a roadway: it reflects what's passing by at the time.

But it is also possible that a theatrical production is not just a mirror of what's around it, but a lamp lit from within. It is not made up of what others thought at the time, but of what had never before been thought, until it was conceived by its makers.

In fact, 'thought' is the wrong word, as theatre artists make a work of art, and not the interpretation of it.

Examples of both ways of looking at a production – as mirror and as lamp – can be illustrated by consideration of Niall Henry's version of *The Playboy of the Western World* at the Peacock Theatre, Dublin, in July 2001. Henry is the artistic director of Blue Raincoat Theatre Company in Sligo. This is truly an ensemble company of actors, four or five of them,

Mikel Murfi as Christy Mahon; Peacock Theatre 2001 (from cover of *the irish review*, autumn 2002)

Photograph: Paul McCarthy

always in training and with the same theatrical background in physical mime; they even follow the teachings of a single French voice theorist and coach. Henry cast as Christy Mahon his Sligo schoolmate, and one of the founders of Barrabas Theatre Company, Mikel Murfi.[7] Murphy trained in Paris in the Jacques Lecoq school.

Cathy Belton was cast as a youthful, sexy Widow Quin, who seduces Christy in a second, but in another second the gormless man loses his concentration. Olwen Fouéré played Pegeen as a not-so-youthful, angry, and intellectually dominant woman, almost like a ballet-master who eventually disciplines the playboy into the strained geometries of a studied *pas de deux*. The pack of village girls are played by Murphy himself, using his fingers as if they were puppets, enacting his juvenile fantasies of girls doting on his handsome face. The village men – Jimmy, Philly, and Michael James – come across as a thick-headed trenchcoated mafia, moving in ominous formation. Movement so much dominates on stage that Synge's language is sometimes rushed or even bungled; sometimes, it is almost ostentatiously disrespected by the actors. In the small Peacock, arranged for transverse staging, it is as if the whole room is the shebeen, and the shebeen is for the time being the whole world, a metaphor for existence itself.

While studying in Paris, Mikel Murfi and Niall Henry saw productions of *The Playboy* at the Chatelet by Japanese companies, Australian companies, and, of course, French companies, all testing their styles upon a world masterpiece. This experience broke the hold over them of Irish traditions of enactment. The company felt free to drop characters, cast against type, alter stage directions, and impose a style that had no precedent in earlier productions of this play, but did arise naturally from the artistic development of the director and the key actors.

If one looks at this 2001 Peacock *Playboy* as a mirror, one may see – as Bill McCormack does – the trench-coated village men as a signifying anachronism, one meant to show that the violence of Irish society brought to light by Synge has its

[7] Arminta Wallace, 'Getting physical with the ghosts of *The Playboy*', *The Irish Times* (14 July 2001).

contemporary manifestation in the Provisional IRA. On the other hand, if one looks at the production as a lamp, one may see some leaders of a still youthful Irish theatrical tradition attaining the confidence to experiment with a sacred text and extend their own powers of self-expression.The thematic point of this *Playboy* seemed to be that the Irish village hates an outsider, and that fear sets off the bullies. But beyond the theme, the company were interested in style: in making something new and beautiful, almost coldly beautiful in form, dedramatized, aesthetic.

There will be readers of this collection who will think it is too much talk about *The Playboy*, and about one Druid production of it in the centennial year of the Abbey that will see another production, this one on the National Theatre stage in June 2004. How to answer except by saying that cultural events are for many (though not everyone) pleasurable and interesting to discuss? Nicholas Grene organized a conference and book of essays at the time of the Murphy season at the Abbey for the 2001 Dublin Theatre Festival. He entitled it *Talking About Tom Murphy*. A very good title…indeed, there should be a new word for a symposium, a *talkabout*. It would evoke that Australian word and liminal event, the walkabout, in which persons deliberately lose their bearings in the vast hinterlands. Their aim is to find out what they are made of, so as to return home knowing old things as if they were new.

PLAYBOYS OF THE PAST

1 | The First *Playboy*

Paige Reynolds

It's Saturday in Dublin, the winter's evening of January 26, 1907. You've purchased a ticket for tonight's production at the Abbey, a double bill of J. M. Synge's *Riders to the Sea* and his new play, a three-act comedy entitled, *The Playboy of the Western World.* The Abbey's a small theatre, smaller at least than the Queen's and other venues that offer popular theatre for audiences of a thousand or more.

Original Abbey Theatre

From Lennox Robinson, Ireland's Abbey Theatre

But tonight the Abbey's packed, with all 562 seats filled. The recent reduction in ticket prices might explain the full house:

tickets in the pit, once priced at a shilling, are now only six pennies. You take your gallery seat, scan the audience, and recognize several playgoers, including Mary Maguire, Francis Sheehy Skeffington and Joseph Holloway, the architect who designed the Abbey, along with reporters from *The Irish Times* and *The Freeman's Journal.* You're eagerly awaiting this new play because you consider Synge particularly talented, having previously appreciated his tragic account of the west in *Riders to the Sea* – though if pressed you might admit that you prefer Lady Gregory's comedies.

Interior of Old Abbey Theatre, during rehearsal

From Christopher Fitz-Simon, The Irish Theatre.

You enjoy both *Riders to the Sea,* and the subsequent orchestral performance. When the curtain rises on Synge's new comedy, you are greeted with a typically realistic western interior, but from the play's opening moments, things seem a little odd. As the first act ends, you and those surrounding you in the gallery are enjoying the comedy, but feel somewhat uneasy with the celebration of the play's young hero, Christy Mahon, for his patricide. During the second act, your discomfort increases, and you hear murmurs among other members of the audience. In the third act, Christy's father appears on-stage, and Christy – as far as you can tell – murders Old Mahon, though the action takes place off-stage. So when Willie Fay, who's playing the role of Christy asserts, 'It's Pegeen I'm seeking only, and what'd I care if you brought me a drift of Mayo girls, standing in their shifts itself maybe, from this place to the Eastern World', you can tolerate no more.[1] This slight to the purity of Irish women

Maire O'Neill (Molly Allgood): The First Pegeen

[1] At this opening performance, Fay mistakenly replaced Synge's phrase 'a drift of chosen females' with the more particular, and thus more inflammatory, reference to 'a drift of Mayo girls.' See Christopher Morash's masterful account of *Playboy*'s opening week in *A History of Irish Theatre 1601-2000* (Cambridge: Cambridge UP, 2002), pp.130-138. My brief accounts of *Playboy*'s opening night and the subsequent week of performances are pieced together from newspaper reports collected in James Kilroy, *The 'Playboy' Riots* (Dublin: Dolmen Press, 1971).

is too egregious. Along with many of your fellow theatregoers, you express disapproval by hissing, stamping, and yelling, noisily overwhelming the remainder of the play.

By asking you to imagine yourself in attendance at *Playboy*'s premiere, I am encouraging you to set aside some of the expectations held by twenty-first-century audience members. As contemporary theatregoers, we are accustomed to regarding direct engagement with the realist stage as unthinkably bad behaviour. Faced with an offensive, or even simply bad, production, a playgoer might mutter a complaint to a companion, roll the eyes in annoyance – but it is quite unlikely that audience members would band together and drown out the dialogue with hisses and shouts of 'kill the author' as they did on this evening in 1907. Yet as alien as *Playboy*'s riotous opening night sounds, this evening at the theatre likely seems in other ways familiar – the anticipation of a new play, the inspection of the audience, the affect elicited by the production. A similar tension between the familiar and the foreign characterized this first production of *The Playboy*: it was, in equal measure, both routine and extraordinary for its audience, who were primed that night to expect stimulating work from a talented and controversial artist.

Unlike Yeats and Gregory, Synge mused only infrequently in public on theatre matters, so no one can be certain of his intentions for this first production of *The Playboy of the Western World*. He may well have anticipated the pleasures and publicity value generated by the audiences' direct engagement with his work; he did, after all, subsequently dub this first production an 'extravaganza'.[2] Whatever his motives, he couched within this entertainment a stark critique of the illusions of societal power held by early twentieth-century audiences and, I would argue, encouraged their riotous responses by luring them into a receptive position in which they might confuse representation and reality.[3] An august body of critics, including many in this

[2] *The Evening Mail*, 29 January 1907, p.2. See *PBR*, p.24

[3] In the volumes of critical work on *Playboy*, a few studies have touched on the important role of audiences and this tension between reality and representation in the play. See Mary King, *The Drama of J.M. Synge*

collection, has long debated not only Synge's aesthetic objectives, but also whether or not he had political intents for this play. It seems to me that in its initial run, *The Playboy of the Western World* worked powerfully – if ultimately, unsuccessfully – to manipulate its first audiences into a critical self-awareness about their authority in both cultural and national politics.

Immediately after this first performance, Gregory wired a telegraph to Scotland, where Yeats was lecturing. It explained simply: 'Audience broke up in disorder at the word shift.'[4] The welter of eyewitness accounts and critical analyses of this first production generally reflect Gregory's concise explanation of why the upheaval occurred: Synge's affront to Irish womanhood – his reference to women's underwear – had so outraged the audience that they felt impelled to protest. There was, of course, much on stage to offend and confuse, and critics have linked the controversy to factors ranging from rising unionist anxiety about Home Rule[5] to a growing awareness of venereal disease.[6] For the most part, however, these appraisals reaffirm the stance of Dubliners who talked about the production in

---

(Syracuse: Syracuse UP, 1985), p.136; J. L. Styan, 'On Playing with the Audience', *The Elements of Drama* (Cambridge: Cambridge UP, 1963), pp.57-63; Edward Hirsch, 'The Gallous Story and the Dirty Deed: The Two Playboys', *Modern Drama* 26, no. 1 (March 1983), reproduced in *Modern Critical Interpretations*: The Playboy of the Western World, ed. Harold Bloom (New York: Chelsea House, 1988), p.112. In her study of *Playboy* and its audiences, Heidi Holder likewise claims that Synge makes it 'quite clear to his audience that their beloved image of the Irish country folk was a mere construction – a construction eminently open to challenge' and it was 'precisely this dismantling of the distinctions between fiction and reality that was the source of Synge's conflict with his audience.' See Heidi Holder, 'Between Fiction and Reality: Synge's *Playboy* and Its Audience', *Journal of Modern Literature* XIV:4 (Spring 1988), p.529.

4 Augusta Gregory, *Our Irish Theatre: A Chapter of Autobiography* (1913; New York: Capricorn Books, 1965), p.112.

5 Lionel Pilkington, *Theatre and the State in Twentieth-Century Ireland: Cultivating the People* (London: Routledge, 2001), p.59.

6 Susan Cannon Harris, *Gender and Modern Irish Drama* (Bloomington: Indiana UP, 2002), pp.69-122.

1907. The Abbey, which professed to be a national theatre, had offered its public an offensive and unflattering picture of Irish peasant life, rather than an affirmative depiction of national folk culture. Consequently, the week-long run of *Playboy* was accompanied not only by vociferous remonstrations, but also by a lively debate about its representations of Irish life and its artistic merit and, hence, about its suitability for performance by the self-proclaimed 'National Theatre Society, Ltd.' – the company run by Gregory, Synge, and Yeats that staged the play.

The ruckus at Saturday's premiere was merely a prelude to further chaos: the theatre was dark on Sunday, but Monday's newspapers offered detailed, if sometimes inaccurate, reports of the play's content and the protests. The second performance on Monday night attracted a small audience of around eighty, seated mostly in the inexpensive pit seats. As soon as the curtain rose on *Playboy*, the audience began stomping its feet, hurling Irish-language invective, and singing refrains from nationalist songs like 'A Nation Once Again'. This same rowdy behaviour characterized Tuesday night. A full house of playgoers, many of whom were not quite sober, ignored Yeats's appeal for a fair hearing for the play and his promises for a fruitful debate the following Monday on 'The Freedom of the Theatre'. After this performance, a brawl erupted in Westmoreland Street. By Wednesday night, crowds gathered in the streets outside the theatre, as hundreds stormed the doors. Strangely, on this evening *The Freeman's Journal* reported that *Riders to the Sea* 'never had a more sympathetic audience'.[7] But when Christy entered the stage, once more the shouts, the skirmishes, and the competing choruses of 'God Save the King' and 'God Save Ireland' began. Audience members trooped through Abbey Street and O'Connell Street after the play, followed closely by the police. By Thursday night, the disturbances decreased and unlike the previous two evenings, no arrests were made. The protests had played themselves out, and the Friday and Saturday performances proceeded smoothly.

---

[7] The Freeman's Journal, 31 January 1907, pp. 7-8. See PBR, p.43.

The audiences for these first productions sometimes have been represented as unenlightened philistines who failed to recognize Synge's genius and attacked his masterpiece for political reasons, much to the surprised dismay of the Abbey directors and performers. But Synge and his cohorts should not be seen sympathetically as the bewildered victims of a nationalist audience's attack. From its inception, the Abbey Theatre placed a great deal of thought and energy into creating a coherent theory of the Irish national audience. Its frequently shifting perceptions of and intentions for these audiences pour out of the promotional, the editorial, and – I would argue – the creative work of its members. This was a theatre that attended to its audiences, even if it refused to welcome what it understood about them. The Abbey associates were aware that Dublin audiences had engaged directly with the stage for centuries: the eighteenth century was rife with theatre riots, like those at Smock Alley, and throughout the nineteenth and early twentieth centuries, audiences had engaged in call-and-response with popular plays, howled at performers, stormed the stage, and shouted down controversial productions, like the 1903 Dublin premiere of Ibsen's *A Doll's House.*[8]

Motivated by a mixture of optimism and hubris, the early Abbey tried to hammer these boisterous audiences into well-behaved spectators who would adhere to bourgeois norms. The architecture of the Abbey directed and focused the spectator's vision toward its proscenium stage, as did its practice of darkening the theatre. In the Abbey's occasional publications and from its stage, Yeats regularly lectured audience members,

---

[8] For a brief account of this 1903 premiere, see Joseph Holloway, *Impressions of a Dublin Playgoer*, 22 August 1903, reproduced in *Laying the Foundations 1902-1904*, eds. Robert Hogan and James Kilroy, vol. 2, *Modern Irish Drama: A Documentary History*, ed. Robert Hogan (Dublin: Dolmen Press, 1976), p.65. Helen M. Burke provides a rich study of eighteenth-century Irish audiences and their behaviour at sites such as Smock Alley in her *Riotous Performances: The Struggle for Hegemony in the Irish Theatre, 1712-1784* (Notre Dame: University of Notre Dame Press, 2003).

demanding they arrive promptly, sit quietly, and not ruffle their programmes during performances. Nonetheless, Irish audiences had forced the Abbey, early in its career, to acknowledge that they were not a passive body in full sway of the dramatic spectacle on hand. From its inception, the institution had a troubled history with controversial plays and rowdy theatre-goers. Yeats's *The Countess Cathleen* (1899), for instance, had been hissed during its first performance owing to its depiction of a woman who sold her soul; and Synge's *In the Shadow of the Glen* (1902) had elicited jeers and had even driven Maud Gonne from the theatre for what she perceived as the play's slurs on Irish women. The Abbey grudgingly came to recognize that its audiences were sometimes antipathetic, raucously antipathetic, to their work.

It seems the Abbey's management anticipated a similarly spirited response to *Playboy*. Prior to the opening, rehearsals were held in secret, an unusual practice for the theatre. Mary Maguire Colum recalled that during these two weeks of rehearsal, 'reports spread through Dublin that there were improprieties in the play and that the womanhood of Ireland was being slandered, and these rumors were received with hilarity by some, with solemnity by others'.[9] Meanwhile, the theatre management and performers expressed anxieties about how the public might respond to *Playboy*'s rough language. Gregory compensated for these concerns by encouraging Yeats to remove his play *The Pot of Broth* from the evening's bill and by replacing it with Synge's popular one-act *Riders to the Sea.* Additionally, both Yeats and Gregory made arrangements to go abroad for the premiere, though only Yeats succeeded in missing the first performance.

In studies of historical popular culture in America, England, and Ireland, scholars often attribute the vociferous engagement of audiences with the stage to their conflation of reality and

[9] Mary Maguire Colum, *Life and the Dream: Memories of a Literary Life in Europe and America* (London: Macmillan & Co., 1947), p.137.

representation.[10] The first production of *Playboy*, it appears, actually encouraged the audience to confuse the real world and the fictive world. Padraic Colum credited this mistake to the play's visual realism, and in particular to the graphic image of Old Mahon's reappearance; according to Colum, this figure with a 'horribly bloodied bandage about his head ... took the whole thing out of the atmosphere of comedy'.[11] *The Irish Times* praised both the play's ' "remorseless truth" in characterization' and its uncannily accurate duplication of peasant speech, even as it acknowledged that Dubliners 'will not publicly approve of the indiscriminate use of the Holy Name on every possible occasion'.[12] Meanwhile, the Abbey actress Maire nic Shiubhlaigh ascribed the audience's upset to Synge's direction, claiming roles were 'played seriously, almost sombrely, as though each character had been studied and its nastiness made apparent'.[13] The realism of the production encouraged its audiences to ignore the fourth wall, and believe they could somehow alter the course of events on stage.

Accounts of the riots underscore the notion that the audience mistook representation for reality and, consequently, conflated the stage and the stalls. On Wednesday night, for instance, when the third act began and Philly declared, 'There will be right sport before night will fall', one press account asserted,

---

10 Elaine Hadley, Melodramatic Tactics: Theatricalized Dissent in the English Marketplace, 1800-1885 (Stanford: Stanford UP, 1995); Lawrence W. Levine, Highbrow/Lowbrow: The Emergence of Cultural Hierarchy in America (Cambridge: Harvard UP, 1988); Stephen Watt, Joyce, O'Casey, and the Irish Popular Theatre (Syracuse: Syracuse UP, 1991).

11 Padraic Colum, *The Road Round Ireland* (New York: Macmillan, 1926), p.368.

12 'Public Amusements: Abbey Theatre', *The Irish Times*, 28 January 1907, p.7. See *PBR*, pp. 11-12.

13 Maire nic Shiubhlaigh, *The Splendid Years* (Dublin: James Duffy, 1955), p.81. In Nic Shiubhlaigh's assessment, Dublin audiences correctly attributed this 'nasty' characterization to Synge's efforts to retaliate for the poor reception of *The Shadow of the Glen* and *The Well of the Saints*.

'This was so very apropos to the exciting situation that all parties in the theatre joined in an outburst of hearty laughter'.[14] The sport, obviously, refers both to the 'sport' that the fictive Mayo community engages in on stage and to the boisterous 'sport' found in the Abbey, which was filled with individuals from the Dublin community primed to support this artful comedy or to protest a play rumoured to slight the Irish. This description also reveals the sheer fun of the protest for its audiences – the playful repartee that night was received with laughter from 'all parties'.

Reports of this first production demand we read the audience's confusion of representation and reality as customary, and their critical response as fairly lighthearted. But nineteenth- and early twentieth-century Irish audiences took quite seriously the authority they possessed to determine how their society would be represented on stage. One source of this logic is easy to understand. In part, the audience acquired this sense of power through the reception contexts of popular melodrama. The three major theatres in Dublin at the turn of the twentieth century – the Theatre Royal, the Gaiety Theatre, and the Queen's Royal Theatre – provided the Irish public with plays by Shakespeare, pantomimes, variety shows, burlesques, and melodramas. Recent scholarship by Cheryl Herr, Stephen Watt, and Mary Trotter indicates that most Dubliners, and in particular the members of the Abbey's fledgling middle-class audience, had fairly significant exposure to the popular theatre, and in particular to melodrama.[15] These audiences had been

---

[14] The Freeman's Journal, 31 January 1907, p.7. See PBR, p.44.

[15] See Séamus de Búrca, The Queen's Royal Theatre, Dublin: 1829-1969 (Dublin: de Búrca, 1983); Cheryl Herr, ed., For the Land They Loved: Irish Political Melodramas, 1890-1925 (Syracuse: Syracuse UP, 1991); Cheryl Herr, Joyce's Anatomy of Culture (Urbana: University of Illinois Press, 1986); Mary Trotter, Ireland's National Theatres: Political Performance and the Origins of the Irish Dramatic Movement (Syracuse: Syracuse UP, 2001); Stephen Watt, Joyce, O'Casey, and the Irish Popular Theatre (Syracuse: Syracuse UP, 1991). In Joyce's Anatomy of Culture, Herr claims, 'everyone followed what went on at the Gaiety, at the Queen's, and at Dan

encouraged, even explicitly asked, by the popular theatre to police the stage. For instance, an 1889 full-page advertisement for Dan Lowrey's Theatre of Varieties promised its entertainments would be 'ABSOLUTELY FREE FROM ALL OBJECTIONABLE FEATURES' and invited the audience to challenge and report 'any suggestive or offensive word or action upon the Stage that may have escaped the notice of the Management.'[16]

No surprise then that the audience responded to *Playboy*'s unsettling depictions of peasant culture so ferociously, particularly since the iconography and thematic concerns of the popular theatre ricocheted through Synge's play. Yet even as *Playboy* invoked these tropes to engage theatregoers, the play challenged its audiences to look critically at their perceived authority through its depiction of the Mayo villagers.

At all times in the play, state law is represented as oblivious to and uninterested in the local community, and thus its citizens regard the police as somewhat ineffectual. They repeatedly depict those who wield a disciplinary mandate merely as a source of amusement, rather than as the central enforcers of law and morality. Sara Tansey, for instance, describes various legal authorities as among the 'wonders of the western world' (105), and the 'jailor and the turnkey' (151) provide little more than fodder for Michael James's drunken ballad.[17] With such absent and impotent officials, the community assumes responsibility for enforcing the law and morality.

While this seems a democratic ideal, in Synge's hands, it turns to mayhem, largely because the community misperceives itself as an audience, a body predicated on its consumption of

---

Lowrey's' (p.96) and the attendance figures she reports in For the Land They Loved support this claim.

16 Reproduced in Herr, *Joyce's Anatomy of Culture* 202-203.

17 All references to Playboy's text are cited parenthetically within the paper. See J. M. Synge, The Playboy of the Western World, J. M. Synge Collected Works, general ed. Robin Skelton, vols. 1-4, Plays: Book 2, ed. Ann Saddlemyer (Washington D. C.: Catholic University of America Press, 1982).

an event or cultural product. The Mayoites crave entertainment from the exercise of authority; they almost always translate justice into spectacle. After Pegeen Mike (played in the first production by Synge's fiancée, Maire O'Neill) recognizes Christy as a liar and turns against him, her greatest pleasure seems to derive from the public nature of his punishment before an audience.

Maire O'Neill (Molly Allgood) as Pegeen Mike.

Colin Smythe Collection

As she exclaims, 'now the world will see him pandied, and he an ugly liar was playing off the hero and the fright of men!' (163). Christy's public punishment will establish, according to her, a truth about his identity otherwise unavailable. Pegeen's representation of Christy's punishment as spectacle is not unique; this same mechanism for understanding civic authority can be found among all the villagers. When the Widow Quin encounters Old Mahon for the first time, she warns Christy to avoid the power of the law because 'it'd be a poor thing to see a judge in his black cap reading out his sentence on a civil warrior the like of you' (125). Her admonition transforms the verdict from the real possibility of Christy's incarceration by English authorities into a pathetic exhibition offered by the juridical system to spectators like herself.

Neither are poets and performers immune from this confusion between reality and representation. When the villagers eventually attempt to convey him to the authorities, Christy similarly imagines his trial as a spectacle. Just as Pegeen Mike imagined his public castigation before an audience, Christy begins thinking of 'his royal judgement looking on the trembling jury in the courts of law' (171). While fantasizing about his audience of a 'trembling jury', Christy shares his death fantasy with the Mayoites who once celebrated him. He imagines that his death sentence will generate a response not unlike that elicited by a tear-jerking melodrama. Evidently, Christy regards his execution primarily as a type of theatre generating pathos among his audience, one that might inspire an opus of celebratory ballads. He describes his death by asserting, 'And won't there be crying out in Mayo the day I'm stretched upon the rope with ladies in their silks and satins snivelling in their lacy kerchiefs, and they rhyming songs and ballads on the terror of my fate?' (171). In this world, punishment and death are staged largely to entertain an audience, and only secondarily to uphold a shaky set of civic standards. Notably, the imminent threat of his demise also leads Christy to misapprehend the audience for his death: where, for instance, will he draw these affluent female spectators from and who, other than himself, has command of poetic métier?

Despite their many thoughtful exegeses concerning Irish audiences, Synge and the Abbey similarly misread – or wilfully ignored – their audiences for this first production. During rehearsals, Synge dismissed the actor's anxieties about the play's language, even as he made small revisions to his script. More dramatically, the Abbey management misunderstood and disregarded how audiences might respond to English authority being called to subdue Irish citizens in their own national theatre. During the first productions of *Playboy*, audiences sought to enforce their authority and punish the Abbey for its offences against the nation. When playgoers began to disrupt the performances on Monday night, Fay threatened to request police protection – the police arrived that night, but were dismissed; but on Tuesday night, Gregory and Yeats called in the Dublin Metropolitan Police to restrain and eject protestors. Yet the audience, like the characters on stage, appeared to regard authorities and their targets as merely another source of entertainment. The audience refused to acknowledge the police as a disciplinary agent with meaningful power, a point made obvious by the many accounts that theatricalize the authorities and their actions. One newspaper headline, for instance, described the riots by announcing, 'POLICE ACTED IN DUMB SHOW'.[18] This headline, like many other reports of the protests, suggests that the audience regarded the officers as per-formers they could effectively dismiss by shouting down – even as the police, at Yeats's request, arrested the rowdier protestors.

The widely accepted understanding that social control was located in the like-minded audience was expressed by one Belfast paper, which demanded the play be withdrawn since 'the public are the jury, and their verdict must be accepted'.[19] This assessment cited the audience – not the theatre, nor the state – as the legitimate source of authority and discipline in the Abbey. Yet the true arbiter of civic authority was revealed during the trials of those arrested for public disturbance during

---

18 The Freeman's Journal, 29 January 1907, p.7.See PBR, p.16.

19 Irish News and Belfast Morning News, 31 January 1907, p.4. See PBR, p.61.

the week of *The Playboy* riots. The English judge presiding over these court cases demarcated the limits of an audience's authority by asserting:

> the rights of an audience in a theatre were very well defined. They might cry down a play which they disliked, or hiss and booh the actors who depended for their positions on the goodwill of audiences, but they must not act in such a manner as had a tendency to excite uproar or disturbance.[20]

The judge here exposes the false sense of communal power provided by the expression of audience taste in a theatre. Audience members may cry and shout, but they must not create an uproar or disturbance that will disrupt real life. Contrary to any utopian assessments of audience response, the policing of the stage by the audience in fact offers no significant social or political power. Most striking is the judge's claim that the audience's 'censure and approbation, though they might be noisy in expressing it, must not be riotous, and must be the expression of the feeling of the moment. If premeditated by a number of persons combined beforehand to cry down a performance or an actor it became criminal'.[21] This judge condones mere immediate affective response, but any subsequent action suggesting possible evidence of critical thinking is considered a danger by the colonial state, a crime worth prosecuting.

By provoking his audiences, Synge encouraged them to manifest an affective connection to the play that transcended passive appreciation. He persuaded his audiences to police *Playboy*, and allowed them to suppose that they held a measure of control not simply over the play's content, but over events in real life as well. Of course, while he might have predicted that audiences would challenge this first production of *Playboy*, he likely did not imagine that his comedic representation of justice as theatre would be faithfully mimicked in the riots and the

---

[20] 'Abbey Theatre Scenes', *The Evening Herald*, 31 January 1907, p.2. See *PBR*, p.52.

[21] ibid.

subsequent trials of protestors. To those of us looking back on the first production, this dynamic between reality and representation offered its audiences a remarkable cautionary tale. Both the Mayo citizens and Abbey audiences misperceived important differences between reality and representation. The citizens of Synge's Mayo could disregard the police with little consequence, but in real life these authorities remained a palpable and brutal threat for the colonized Irish – one that could not simply be jeered off the streets. As such, the first production and the events surrounding it insisted that the Abbey's audience distinguish between the theatre of the state and the state of the theatre. That this critique played out on the stage, stalls, newspages, streets, and courts is, I would argue, one of central reasons we still, almost a century later, marvel at the first *Playboy*.

2 | Belfast Said 'No' to *The Playboy*

Ophelia Byrne

UPROAR IN A DUBLIN THEATRE

AN IRISH PLAY RESENTED

MR SYNGE'S DISGUSTING TRAVESTY

DIALOGUE FULL OF BLASPHEMY

A HANDFUL OF FILTH

AN ABOMINATION

ROTTEN AND REPULSIVE PIECE PERFORMED UNDER CASTLE PROTECTION

SPECIAL TELEGRAM, DUBLIN, MONDAY

SPECIAL TELEGRAM, DUBLIN, TUESDAY NIGHT

It is fair to say that Belfast said 'no' to *ThePlayboy*. 'The play', reported the unionist *Belfast Newsletter* with masterly understatement, 'had a very mixed reception ... The dialogue is ... full of oaths and blasphemy.'[1] The nationalist *Irish News* declared *The Playboy*, rather wonderfully, a 'wretched, dunderheaded farrago of blasphemy, obscenity and caricature ....'[2]

---

[1] 'Uproar in a Dublin Theatre', *Belfast Newsletter*, January 29, 1907, p.7.

[2] 'Pegeen Mike – a Parricide – Personalities – and Pretences', *Irish News*, Jan. 31, 1907, p.4.

This echoed southern receptions, where the unionist *Irish Times* frowned at *The Playboy*'s language, whilst the nationalist *Freeman's Journal* had vituperative fits at the play in general. The two seem similar narratives, then, and to assume an early shared *Playboy* history between Dublin and Belfast appears reasonable.

Thereafter, if anything, Belfast seemed to react with less intensity than Dublin. Early touring productions received a lacklustre response in Belfast, while the play does not appear to have been staged by a Belfast-based company until 1926[3]. Mid-century it was only sporadically produced by northern professsional companies, with *The Playboy* then noted to be welcome, but 'beginning to feel his age a bit'[4]; musical versions such as *The Heart's a Wonder* adapted by Nuala and Mairin O'Farrell proved quite popular, as did visiting productions featuring stars such as Siobhán McKenna. Later and up to the present, the piece has been and is professionally produced periodically, being promoted as an appealing comedy classic with no remarkable effect.

On balance, then, it seems fair to conclude that *Playboy* is not a significant part of the northern canon, and that the Dublin story is the whole story. The northern record seems merely a footnote to the larger one, a history of absence rather than presence. But absence, in itself, can be telling: the silent voice in history is sometimes the loudest. So is it justified to simply include Belfast history with that of the mainstream? Or is there a reason why *Playboy* in the north is not a significant part of the canon? And if so, how does the production history, or lack of it, illuminate differences and similarities between northern and southern theatre history as a whole?

---

[3] The Northern Drama League production appears to be the first, at the Central Hall, Rosemary Street, Belfast, on December 19, 1926; the play had a good audience, and a critic noted that it was 'some years since it was previously seen in this city, the last occasion being when it was presented by the Abbey Players'. ('Northern Drama League', *Irish News,* November 18, 1925).

[4] 'The Group' fans "Playboy's" flickering flame', *Belfast Newsletter*, November 13, 1957, p.4.

In answering these questions, revisiting Belfast's responses to the play's premiere production is instructive. If on the surface so similar to those in Dublin, on closer inspection they prove in fact quite different: Belfast said 'no' in its own way. In the case of the Unionist community, the *Playboy* opening coincided with the second annual meeting of the newly formed Ulster Unionist Council, predominantly concerned with the possibility of the loathed Home Rule by the back door. Hence, though factual accounts of the *Playboy* debacle and subsequent court cases appeared in the unionist papers in the north, precious leader columns and commentary space were otherwise reserved. The worry was English perceptions of Home Rule and Ireland, not a play in Dublin; the northern unionist community largely did not engage on the *Playboy* issue.

Nationalists differed. Many inches of angry northern nationalist column space[5] were devoted to the *Playboy*'s declared 'gross libel upon the Irish peasantry';[6] as in Dublin, the play was directly related to the issue of Home Rule, being viewed as potentially harmful to mass perception abroad. 'If Connaught could be peopled with popular parricides and their admirers for the benefit of foolish Ulster Unionists and credulous English people', fumed the *Irish News,* Home Rule opponents would 'have an easy task when they begin to prove that Ireland is lawless and unfit for Self-Government'[7]. The danger was that the stage could be peopled with parricides, and if merely boycotted, the play could then be toured abroad with 'the hallmark of Irish Metropolitan approval'[8]. Protest rather than mere boycott was essential to stop this travesty.

---

[5] It was said the play used language 'from England … originally coined in London slums and then developed in the atmosphere of military barracks' ('Twice a Week', *Irish News*, January 30, 1907, p.5), and that the *Playboy* portrayed 'a far more objectionable type of character than even the sots and buffoons of the last two or three generations' ('Ireland on the Stage', *Irish News*, Feb. 4, 1907, p.4).

[6] 'An Alleged Irish Comedy', *Irish News,* January 29, 1907, p.5.

[7] 'Twice a Week', *Irish News,* January 30, 1907, p.5.

[8] 'Ireland on the Stage', *Irish News,* February 4, 1907, p.4.

There, however, the similarity between nationalist responses north and south ends. For nationalist Belfast next appeared to use *The Playboy* as a sort of theatrical frontline, one by which it could clearly distinguish itself from its southern brethren. Coverage of the play tellingly contrasted the city's own Ulster Literary Theatre, founded in 1904, with the Abbey – and it was the Abbey which was found wanting. Ulster Literary Theatre members were thought 'pure of mind and heart and truly Irish in their instincts'[9]; a letter from 'National Theatre' to the *Irish News* stated:

> I am glad that here in Belfast we have a young and prospering Irish Theatre, which has a clearer and cleaner conception of art than the decadents of Dublin. The Ulster Literary Theatre is a society of which Belfast may well be proud: it need not fear that it will ever be guilty of such a gross insult to public morality as *The Playboy of the Western World* even though it lacks the support of such distinguished persons as W.B. Yeats, Lady Gregory and Mr. Edward Martyn.[10]

The contrasts are clearly stated: Belfast is moral; Dublin decadent. Belfast is young and prospering; Dublin, by implication is old and mouldering. Dublin cannot have confidence in its theatre; Ulster can. And Dublin may have the support of distinguished personages, but Belfast, at least cannot be led astray. Its theatre is at one with itself: if unsupported by Dublin's *hoi polloi*, it knows what it is and what it stands for. And in that, Belfast has no doubt whatsoever.

If the passage is notable for the strength of the delineation, there is also a patent hurt sense of abandonment. But most notable of all is the utter sense of confidence. Belfast is declaring its self-sufficiency and self-reliance; in this, the community clearly expects theatre to play its part. And of what that part comprises, there is no question. For if both the nationalist and unionist responses to *The Playboy* speak of anything, it is

---

[9] 'Pegeen Mike – a Parricide – Personalities – and Pretences', *Irish News*, Jan 31, 1907, p.4.

[10] 'Letter from 'National Theatre', 'Riders to the – ?', in 'The Public Forum', *Irish News*, Jan. 31, 1907, p.6.

control. The play provides a rare public moment in which, consciously or not, both communities express their understanding of the parameters within which theatre will work. Nationalists may do this in words, unionists by denying theatre power in refusing to engage with it, but each asserts something similar: theatre will not act beyond the constraints placed upon it by the community.

Yet to say this, as does the nationalist writer cited, with such abundant confidence at the height of the Dublin debacle, seems extraordinary. For just as in Dublin, Belfast's Literary Theatre was a serious one. Founded to do original indigenous work, it too was highly principled and ambitious. So why, in the teeth of the *Playboy* riots, was there northern confidence rather than anxiety that its theatre would not follow suit? Seek to itself stage *The Playboy*? Or even find its own version?

One answer was National Theatre's suggestion of superior morals; another may be that community leaders, whether consciously or not, knew that if morality failed then socio-political factors would fill in the gaps. In Belfast, these comprised a complex cocktail of morality, religion and politics; held in this vice-like grip, a *Playboy*-style theatre debacle would be well nigh impossible. It is arguable, of course, that such unwritten control is not uncommon for theatre; Yeats, through *The Playboy,* was arguing this very point regarding theatre in Dublin. There, he believed, the artform was facing the unwritten censorship of the majority community; struggling against unendurable circumstances, it must make its stand for freedom of thought. What the Belfast *Playboy* experience shows however, is the relativism of this position. Viewed in isolation, certainly, the Dublin situation seems both difficult and intransigent: there are two sides, two opinions, two communities at complete loggerheads. Viewed in terms of Belfast, however, Dublin can be alternately viewed as fertile ground, ripe for exploitation and cultivation by an astute political operator seeking to generate dialogue. For looked at comparatively, Yeats went to battle his apparently impossible circumstances rather well armed.

First, theatre was already an established tradition in Dublin, and the city the centre of a very marked literary movement;

northern practitioners noted that there, 'a national theatre was bound to find many supporters from the first'.[11] Next, Dublin's public space was relatively uncontested. Its population was majority Roman Catholic, comprising 84% of Dublin's population in 1899,[12] and in scale had changed only sluggishly in the pre-*Playboy* period.[13] Third, there was finance. The northern nationalist press might disdainfully note the support of 'the English lady' whose name they 'forgot', and who 'found'[14] the money for the Abbey, but they did so knowing private sponsorship gave artistic independence to a degree. Fourth, there was patronage: the Irish Literary Theatre's opening programme 'gave prominent feature to the theatre's high proportion of titled guarantors'.[15] Finally, there was the leadership of Lady Gregory and W.B. Yeats, who as Ascendency or quasi-Ascendency figures connected to the establishment élite, could – just – shield controversial work from its detractors.

Small as these advantages might have been, they are thrown into sharp relief by the northern experience. Relatively speaking, the Ulster Literary Theatre (ULT) had very little. Begun by members of the small Protestant National Association to spread the ideals and principles of Wolfe Tone and the United

---

11 J.W., 'The Ulster Literary Theatre', *Uladh, a Literary and Critical Magazine,* Feil Brighde, February 1905, p.4.

12 J.V. O'Brien, *Dear Dirty Dublin: A City in Distress,* (Berkeley, CA: University of California Press, 1982), pp.282-3. Cited in Lionel Pilkington, *Theatre and the State in Twentieth-Century Ireland: Cultivating the People* (London: Routledge, 1981), p.6.

13 With its industries in decline, Dublin had a population of 245,000 in 1891, representing a fall from the mid century's figure of 258,000. The Greater Dublin population figure was heftier, at 347,000, but this figure was debated; Belfast noted acidly that it was only by constantly redrawing the city's boundaries that Dublin could remain ahead. See Clarkson, Leslie. 'The City and the Country', in *Belfast: the Making of the City* [Hereafter: *BMC*], eds. J.C. Beckett et al. (Belfast: Appletree Press, 1988, 1983), p.161.

14 'Twice a Week', *Irish News,* Jan 30, 1907, p.5.

15 Pilkington, Lionel. *Theatre and the State in Twentieth-Century Ireland: Cultivating the People* (London: Routledge, 1981), p.7.

Irishmen, the ULT faced a myriad of problems, not least the issue at stake in the *Playboy* debates: use of, and control over, theatre as a public space. Belfast at this time was growing by leaps and bounds, and more rapidly so at this time than any other city in the British Isles. The population rose from 20,000 in 1800 to 75,000 in 1841; just fifty years later, in 1901, it stood at an incredible 349,000.[16] And with such change came another: shifting religious demographics. At a time when religious affiliation was 'increasingly a badge of social identification',[17] Belfast, a cradle of Presbyterianism from its early years, now experienced an influx of Catholics, rising from a tenth of the population at the beginning of the century to one quarter by the end.[18] If this left it still a very Protestant city, it was also one changing rapidly, with inhabitants living cheek by jowl under pressure cooker conditions: the result was massive instability and insecurity, most particularly for the working-classes.

How to cope? One option was segregation. As early as the 1860s, community separateness in Belfast was almost complete – in fact, it had almost assumed what would become its twentieth century form.[19] By 1886 Belfast's first 'tribal' map had been produced; by 1907, at the time of *The Playboy,* those boundaries were being copperfastened.[20] In Marianne Elliott's words, by the turn of the century for example 'most Catholics could attend exclusively Catholic educational establishments, exclusively Catholic public houses, shops and parks, and often even exclusively Catholic workplaces.'[21] But segregation did not always work, as people still lived in close proximity, and when it did not, combustion resulted. Sectarian tension found frequent

---

16 Clarkson, Leslie, in J.C. Beckett, *BMC*, p.153.

17 Collins, Brenda, 'The Edwardian City', in *BMC*, p.73.

18 Clarkson, Leslie, in *BMC*, p.165.

19 Heatley, Fred, 'Community Relations and the Religious Geography, 1800-86', in *BMC*, p.142.

20 Gray, John, City in Revolt: James Larkin and the Belfast Dock Strike of 1907. (Belfast: Blackstaff Press, 1985), p.16.

21 Elliott, Marianne. *The Catholics of Ulster: a History* (London: Allen Lane, 2000), p.326.

expression through violent and often life-threatening riots, and by 1907 these had become a 'recurring feature of life in the town'.[22] Such sectarian riots first occurred in 1832, and thereafter in 1852, 1857, 1864, 1872, 1880, 1884, 1886, 1898 and 1901, each marking an intensification of the previous.[23] These were often extended and brutal: the 1886 riots, for example, lasted four months and resulted in 32 deaths and 371 injuries.[24] If proximity space in such conditions was notoriously combative, shared space was even more so; speeches at the Custom House steps, Belfast's Speaker's Corner, while regularly received with amusement, could often also lead to violence, whilst at football matches spectators could come armed with revolvers.[25] In this, theatre could not prove an exception.

Belfast theatre riots had a long tradition. From the 1798 rebellion onwards, theatres were known as potential sites of disturbances. These were often highly politically nuanced. There are descriptions of unwritten understandings whereby Protestants and Catholics occupied the cheaper seats on different nights,[26] whilst there is evidence that certain plays were bywords for riotous behaviour. Actor Whitford Kane recalled in his autobiography that Boucicault's *The Shaughraun* was always a draw in Belfast:

> not so much for its dramatic value, but because the audience knew it would get a chance to participate .... it generally turned into a battle between the religious factions... The gallery patrons [for example] would point out to the English captain where the young Irish rebel was concealed ... cracking the skull of a fellow citizen during a performance of *The Shaughraun* was hardly a misdemeanour.[27]

---

[22] Heatley, p.137.
[23] Elliott, p.325.
[24] ibid.
[25] Gray, *City in Revolt*, p.17.
[26] ibid.
[27] Kane, Whitford. *Are We All Met?* (London : Elkin, Mathews & Marrot, 1931), pp.23 and 46f, cited in Hagal Mengel and Sam Thompson, *Modern Drama in Ulster*, (Frankfurt am Main: Peter Lang, 1986), p.42.

The period in question was no exception. John Gray tells of an occasion when the Palace Theatre of Varieties had to close when a performer sang *The Wearing of the Green* to the wrong audience; a fusillade of porter bottles and rivets resulted.[28] However it operated, then, theatre was intrinsically political. Nuances were well understood because they had to be, and performer and manager gauged circumstances carefully on a night-by-night basis. Otherwise, they knew the outcome. It was a straightforward fact of life that theatre space in Belfast was contentious, that certain topics were inflammatory, and that their presentation in any format would simply result in a riot.

For those attempting to present serious theatre in Belfast, this presented evident challenges. In a society where virtually everything was politicized, from name and school to street to workplace, to cause a full-blown riot in Belfast would be no achievement. Instead, the issue was how to address many basic topics, even in a serious and earnest manner, *without* causing offence and potential riotous behaviour. To which audience did one appeal? How to walk the tightrope but not just to speak to the 'converted'? Was it possible to reach both communities, and say something meaningful, without causing a riot?

Negotiating this political minefield as they were, some northern theatre practitioners' reactions to the *Playboy* situation were highly cynical. Themselves skilled in assessing political nuances, they firmly believed Yeats had engineered the theatre riots as a house-filling technique, and were incredulous that such means be used. Alice Milligan, a well-known northern nationalist activist and writer, directly accused the Abbey of engaging via the play in the 'new-found art of advertising'. *The Playboy*, she thought, was an 'extravaganza of an advertisement', while Synge she described as merely Yeats' 'sandwich man'.[29] This was reiterated in an *Irish News* piece describing a Critic and a Philistine in discussion at a Belfast theatre; they agree only that the 'Abbey Theatre question' should not be discussed, for

---

[28] Gray, p.17.

[29] 'Letter from Miss Alice Milligan', *Freeman's Journal*, February 4, 1907, p.4.

as the Philistine says, 'It would be rather like flogging a dead horse, wouldn't it? Synge has got his advertisement, and there's an end on't.'[30]

Such 'advertisements', if indeed they were such, were not open to the Belfast theatricals in their extremely politicized climate. It was a struggle, however, to work out what was. In theatre terms, Belfast was plain hard work. The impressive new Grand Opera House, opened to be Belfast's home of proper drama in 1895, had closed as such in 1904, being transformed instead into a Palace of Varieties offering fare more attractive to the teeming industrial masses. *The Belfast Critic* concluded gloomily that 'Belfast in its relations to theatrical affairs is a city by itself'[31]; certainly, it was a city still nervous regarding theatre. This was not solely because of the possibility of riots, though they cannot have helped; as significant was the fact that theatre had long been campaigned against by the clergy and was now 'rather suspect'.[32] A mid-century letter to the press signed by every clergyman of the established church in Belfast, had declared that drama was

> the most dangerous part of our literature. Throughout the entire range of all plays an anti-Christian principle is maintained. ... All the accompaniments are objectionable, the hours, the assembly, the excitement.[33]

The impact of this opposition has been thought 'lasting, and acutely damaging'.[34] It is suggested, for example, that the ULT policy of anonymity arose from 'the attitude of certain sections of Belfast public opinion to "playactors" ';[35] Marion Crimmons, an actress, declared: 'I got on because I wasn't very religious,

---

30 'At An Irish Play', *Irish News,* February 7, 1907, p.8.

31 The Playgoer in *The Belfast Critic,* November 10, 1900.

32 Hewitt, John. ' "The Northern Athens" and after', in *BMC,* p.74.

33 Cited by Hempton, David and Myrtle Hill, *Evangelical Protestantism in Ulster Society, 1740-1890* (London : Routledge, 1992), p.117.

34 Gray, John, 'Popular Entertainment', in J.C. Beckett, p.107. (Cf. footnote 13).

35 Sam Hanna Bell, *The Theatre in Ulster* (Totowa, N.J.: Rowman and Littlefield, 1972), p.36.

and it wasn't a sin to play on the stage'.[36] In Belfast, it was said, 'the theatre is not recognized but merely tolerated'[37]; contemporaneous accounts tell of those who 'would as soon visit the infernal regions'[38] as the theatre.

This helps to explain why the ULT had so few of the Abbey's comparative practical advantages. The theatre's members were not of the élite, and 'nobody', we are told, 'in the Ulster Theatre had any money worth talking about'.[39] As an entity, the ULT was always broke. With both its politics and its artform out of step with the majority, public appeals in Belfast garnered just five shillings; no Miss Horniman ever appeared, nor did a building. The establishment figures who gave the Abbey its standing also did not emerge; Belfast did not have a resident leisured class, and its élite gave spare time predominantly to charity. If the city had new millionaires, this industrial aristocracy was 'unostentatious'[40] in style, and preferred to 'indulge in conspicuous consumption outside Belfast'.[41] The ULT was consequently in a practical quandary. Lacking patronage, money, sympathy to the artform, or a stable environment, its founders turned south for assistance where, though practitioners might protest or even believe otherwise, theatre in their eyes had a comparatively easier existence. Then, offering their new enterprise as a northern branch of the Irish Literary Theatre, the northerners unexpectedly hit their final problem: W.B. Yeats.

Alone of the Irish National Theatre Society members in being 'haughty and aloof',[42] Yeats refused the offer of a

---

36 ibid., p.39.

37 J.W., 'The Ulster Literary Theatre', *Uladh, a Literary and Critical Magazine,* Feil Brighde, February 1905, p.4.

38 Harry Furniss writing in *Black and White* in 1891.Cited by John Gray, 'Popular Entertainment', in *BMC,* p.110.

39 ULT member Rutherford Mayne, cited by Bell, *The Theatre in Ulster,* p.51.

40 Gray, *City in Revolt*, p.4.

41 Collins, Brenda., 'The Edwardian City', in J.C. Beckett, *BMC,* p.179.

42 Bulmer Hobson, ULT founder, cited in Bell, p.2.

northern branch out of hand. In this he was at least consistent. In 1897 he had written to Alice Milligan noting the intention to produce 'certain celtic plays', ideally during the 1898 Feis Ceoil which Belfast was hosting, but which he now sought for Dublin to launch the new enterprise. '… We cannot go to Belfast', he noted, 'for we must begin where the Literary Movement has done most to prepare the ground … if the Feis goes [to Belfast] we may be driven to London … '[43] Belfast in Yeats's eyes could be neither home for, nor satellite of, the new movement. This effectively left the ULT abandoned.

Attributed to a reported 'antipathy towards all things Ulster',[44] Yeats's action may conversely be comprehended as a pragmatic move by one already dealing with dissenting nationalist voices in the southern theatre. Artistically, however, the action had major repercussions both in terms of the northern and southern movements. The latter lost a raft of undoubted talent which could have enriched it; people who wished to create work which resonated directly with Ulster audiences and did not want to have to do so via Dublin and perhaps at best, a once-yearly tour. In northern terms, however, Yeats's refusal proved particularly damaging. This went beyond a loss of individual talent, or even wounded pride; in the wider picture, it left the northern company enclosed within local strictures. Without even the embrace of a national movement, or the aesthetic protection of a figure like Yeats, the group was completely at the mercy of local forces. As a consequence, the potential for undoubtedly talented creators to produce *Playboy*-style contentious, cutting-edge, truly difficult work within their own locale was severely curtailed. Northern commentators might well speak with confidence then of the absence of *The Playboy*; for reasons of finance, politics, religion, patronage, and

---

[43] Letter from W.B. Yeats to Alice Milligan, [? 28 July 1897], from Coole Park, in Kelly, John, gen. ed., Gould, Kelly, Toomey eds. *The Collected Letters of W.B. Yeats,* vol. II, 1896-1900, (Oxford: Clarendon Press, 1997), p.128.

[44] Bell, p.2.

isolation, northern theatre was indeed radically controlled in its actions.

The degree of difference in that control – and by inference, that of the relative freedom rather than constriction of Dublin – is amply proven by the reception of *Playboy* itself. The Abbey brought the play to Belfast on the company's second visit to the city, two years after its premiere. This was a daring move, as the company's reception on its very first visit to Belfast's Theatre Royal in December 1908 had not been a success. Though the Abbey's international standing was fervently flagged in advance of this first visit by a proselytizing nationalist press, apparently anticipating a poor response, and *The Playboy* did not feature on the programme, descriptions of the company as the 'ideal National Theatre'[45] were disputed even in the pages of the *Irish News.*[46] The Belfast establishment simply refused its patronage, with the 'yawning vacancies in the fashionable parts'[47] of the house highlighted in general reports of dwindling attendances during the visit. Nationalist and unionist critics alike rejected the company's opening choice of *In the Shadow of the Glen,* the *Irish News* finding it 'not an acceptable picture'[48]of Irish life, and the *Newsletter* declaring 'its ethics … beneath discussion'.[49] *Riders to the Sea* was found uncontroversial and praiseworthy by all, but with drama of a political bent, critics divided on sectarian lines. The *Irish News* offered fulsome praise to Lady Gregory's *The Rising of the Moon*; the *Newsletter* conversely noted that 'We refrain from commenting upon its political aspect'. [50] This

---

[45] 'Irish Plays – Next Week', *Irish News,* November 28, 1908, p.6.

[46] Letter signed 'P.T. MacG', 'About "Ideal" National Drama in The Public Forum', *Irish News,* December 2, 1908, p.6; the argument is that the writer does 'not believe that the ideal of the Irish nation is drama in English'.

[47] Letter signed 'A Supporter of Irish Drama, A Disgusted Belfastian: to the Editor', *Irish News,* December 5, 1908, p.7.

[48] 'Amusements: The Abbey Company at the Theatre Royal', *Irish News,* December 1, 1908, p.3.

[49] 'The Irish Players', *Belfast Newsletter,* December 1, 1908, p.8.

[50] ibid.

'political style of dramatic criticism in Belfast'[51] was itself noted and criticized in the letters pages; with palpable relief, commentators sought refuge in complimenting the performances without the necessity of qualification, and the first visit finally passed over.

Despite this lacklustre first reception, the Abbey again braved Belfast in August 1909. This time *The Playboy* did feature on the programme, the company perhaps hopeful of a sympathetic hearing after Synge's untimely death, and the play's coincidental staging with a significant Belfast Irish Week. If so, the anticipation proved misguided. The expensive seats for *Playboy*'s Belfast premiere were 'very sparsely peopled' indeed, while the popular too 'might have been more largely patronized', the *Irish News* again thought it generally 'a matter for regret ... that a wider interest has not been shown up to the present amongst Belfast people in the Abbey theatre's work'.[52] The play itself won baffled responses, seeming so far beyond the acceptable theatrical frame of reference that critics seemed perplexed as much as outraged at the very fact of its creation. 'The audience last night seemed unable to discover Mr. Synge's motive', mused the *Belfast Newsletter*. 'It is difficult to say what exactly Mr. Synge had in his mind in writing the work.'[53] The nationalist *Irish News* came up with an answer: Synge was a victim of his own dramatic zeal, and the play was consequently regrettable and quite indefensible. But in the main, from the wider community there was no response. Given that the Abbey was a company of influence both nationally and internationally, the company saw no public protests in Belfast, but Belfast had other ways to make its thinking clear. The play was staged, desultorily attended, saw a 'flavouring of "boohs" '[54] as well as

---

[51] Letter signed 'Simple Thespian', 'The Play, and the Critics: to the Editor', *Irish News,* December 4, 1908, p.7.

[52] 'Abbey Theatre Company', *Irish News,* August 4, 1909, p.5.

[53] 'Grand Opera House: 'The Playboy of the Western World', Belfast Newsletter, Aug. 4, 1909.

[54] 'Abbey Theatre Company', *Irish News,* August 4, 1909, p.5.

applause from those present, but was in the main ignored. Belfast did not engage, and the play moved on.

This Belfast reception of *Playboy* serves to highlight the most crucial comparative difference between making theatre in Belfast and Dublin at this time: the possibility of change. In the south, Lionel Pilkington has suggested, the National Theatre rehearsed, and to some extent anticipated in its works the future political organization of Irish society.[55] *Playboy* is in these terms part of a larger negotiation taking place. The minority southern unionist community is beginning to negotiate its place in the context of possible majority self-government, and *Playboy* reflects and rehearses this action. Understood thus, Nationalists might still view the play as an effort by the southern Ascendancy-associated unionist minority to attack their very essence. Southern unionists might still view it as their 'Belfast letter', defending minority individualism in the face of majority 'mob' rule. But crucially, in either case, there is an imaginative engagement of sorts on the issue of home rule for Ireland, in whatever measure, by both parties.

Such acknowledgement was not even beginning in Belfast. Terence Dooley speaks of a 'divide between Ulster and southern Unionists …'[56] with those of Ulster being distinguished from their southern counterparts by adherence 'to the more rigidly defined concept of the union, to be enforced by armed struggle if necessary'.[57] As they comprised the overwhelming majority of the Belfast population, the city was not even beginning to think in terms of imagining the possibility of change. Belfast's theatrical negotiations were thus by necessity at a far rawer level: rather than the future of an emerging Ireland, they simply attempted to get two different traditions to sit together in the same space, to experience each other as part of the same community, and to see the effect of their lack of

---

55 Lionel Pilkington, *Theatre and the State in Twentieth-Century Ireland: Cultivating the People* (London: Routledge, 1981), p.37.

56 Terence Dooley, *The Decline of the Big House in Ireland* (Dublin: Wolfhound Press, 2001), p.222.

57 ibid., p.218.

negotiation. The broad topics ULT plays addressed were not the potent cocktail of religion and sexuality – sexuality is still very rarely focused on in theatre in Ulster – but those of religion and space. Most often, the plays dealt in the most basic elements of everyday life including work, language, and home, showing their politicization and its problematic effects most often through humour. These works were hugely successful, carefully coded and knew how far to go. On one occasion, for example, the theatre manager asked the actors:

> not to let off too strong… because he had been informed that there were men up there who had been told that this play made fun of a certain Order, and that they were all lined up with rivets and bolts in their pockets. But we started off with *The Drone* and they got into really good humour with the result that when *Thompson* came on, instead of bolts and nuts and so forth landing on the stage, I never heard a play receive such acclamation.[58]

The Abbey plays, with their radically different sphere of operation, were negotiating in other circumstances. The visits of the company to Belfast with works such as *Playboy* prove the degree of difference between the two, and the impossibility of its transference. To plunge that *modus operandi* operation into a city with a very different form of reference was impracticable; the city would simply refuse to engage. *Playboy* was part of a whole different negotiation.

Hence, *Playboy*'s early Belfast history cannot be subsumed into the mainstream. Instead, it acts as an undertow, compelling in itself and counterpointing the other. It confirms that the apparent difficulties in Dublin were only comparative; despite the apparent bitterness of the *Playboy* debacle, in Dublin such acrimony in fact heralds change and development. In Belfast, conversely, the play's early productions confirm a trenchancy, a digging in, and the necessity for Belfast theatre of finding a way of peopling the no-man's-land between. It also serves to explain the play's absence. In the immediate years to come even the

[58] Playwright Rutherford Mayne on a production of *Thompson in Tír na nÓg* by Gerald Macnamara, cited by Bell, p.44.

Abbey gave up the *Playboy* attempt, its subsequent Belfast tours in 1910, 1912 and 1918 leaving the play off their programmes. Later, Ulster theatre would confirm its own distinctive early turn, in taking its own line to that of Dublin. *The Playboy* would still be periodically produced, but other crucial measures of northern similarity, difference and change would emerge.

Today, it might be argued that the fault-lines *The Playboy* exposed for the theatre in Ulster are still present, even now. The idea of producing drama which critiques the other community, as did Synge, remains very difficult, and the issue of careful balance is very real. There are single-identity dramas which depict affectionate, thoughtful and sometimes critical portrayals of one community or the other, by a member of that community. Critical drama addressing both traditions tends to follow the ULT line of plaguing both houses. More controversially, there have been a small number of dramas where balance has been ignored. Extreme controversy and front-page headlines have resulted.

And yet even the periodically attempted critiques which have emerged are not the same as *The Playboy*. They have typically focused on the establishment or its representatives, and not on the lived daily reality of the other community itself. To paint a severely critical dramatic picture of the actual community not one's own remains largely taboo. To that end, *The Playboy* remains a curiosity in northern terms. The principle of negotiation it provoked in Dublin – that of two communities arguing but simultaneously imagining their way through to a shared future in whatever political format – has in northern theatre terms not yet taken place. In that way, it might be said that Belfast's own *Playboy* has never really happened. That kind of conversation or negotiation has at grassroots level yet really to begin.

3 | The Playboy IN the Western World: J. M. Synge's Play in America

John Harrington

One of the remarkable qualities of that remarkable play, *The Playboy of the Western World*, is that it dramatizes a very localized and unified vision to very broad and diversified audiences. It has often been pointed out that the rousing reception it received in Dublin in 1907 was to some degree caused by the resentment felt by middle-class and urban spectators who were in fact unfamiliar with what Synge described as 'a wild coast of Mayo' and at the same time offended by his image of western Ireland. There is, as the play shows memorably, a great gap between a gallous tale and a dirty deed, and there are also great gaps associated with the play suggested by its inspiration of parallel texts such as Mustapha Matura's *The Playboy of the West Indies*. There ways in which this curious dynamic in *The Playboy of the Western World* between the local and the cosmopolitan is textual: the script, for example, for all its microscopic analysis of Mayo, manages to mention Liverpool, California, France, and Norway. However, the nature of dramatic performance creates even greater gaps for the play to bridge, beginning with that between the west and Dublin in 1907 and continuing through a very long record of international performances through the twentieth century.

A lively part of that record has to do with the long history of Synge's play in America, which involves that great Transatlantic gap that takes many forms other than miles. For example, one justly forgotten chapter in that history, one suggestive of gaps, was, in 1978, a musical adaptation of *The Playboy* called *Back Country*, perhaps in emulation of *Oklahoma!*. Book and lyrics were by Jacques Levy, who transferred the setting to West Kansas, giving a new spin to the idea of 'the Western World'. He rechristened Shaun Keogh as Floyd Beavis, and also renamed the Widow Quin as Lucy Jane DeRambeau Finletter, whose big number is the song 'All the Men in My Life'. *Back Country* closed in Boston. This particular doomed production is not of any great significance in itself, but it is a representative part of a pattern of treatments of Synge's play and of great transatlantic cultural discommunications. Similar illustrations include an earlier musical adaptation in 1971 called *Christy*, in which, in performance, as Mel Gussow of the *New York Times* reported, 'accents waver all the way from Erin to Brooklyn (as in 'is youse the man who killed yer father?')'. More recently, in 1996, the play was revived in Los Angeles, which is rather further west than Mayo in many senses, and the readers of *Variety* were told that it was about conflict between 'a young, distraught potato farmer' and 'Pegeen Mike's wimpy cousin Shawn'.

There is nothing particularly wrong with these genuinely spirited approaches to the play, and nothing particular to praise in 'faithful' productions as a new and inflexible orthodoxy. But the results over time document a cultural history that may be important to the play's future. I have no doubt whatsoever that *The Playboy of the Western World* will have as exciting a twenty-first century history as it did a twentieth century one. However, recent academic critics, and I include myself among them, have spent much more energy dissecting the *Playboy* opening in Dublin 1907 or in America in 1911 than we have looked at it over time and distance, or, as the statisticians have it, 'longitudinally'. No better subject for that kind of analysis than *The Playboy*, because production history documents a transformation over time of Synge's play from an abrasive polemic into, especially in American hands, a cloying comedy of indeterminate import. Christopher Murray, in *Twentieth Century*

Irish Drama: Mirror up to Nation, has called *The Playboy* the *Hamlet* of modern Irish drama; he did so more for the quantity of critical discussion than for the interesting parallel his comparison provokes between the late-arriving 'real' Hamlet and the late-arriving 'real' Christy. However, it is equally interesting to consider the play as *The Tempest* of modern Irish drama. *The Tempest* has endured an equally radical transformation, rather in the reverse direction, from an elaborate and decorative wedding masque into an essay on race and colonization. In contrast, *The Playboy* has, in the 20th century, lost rather than acquired political edge, and that becomes a defining condition of its future in the 21st century.

Ideally, production histories in performing arts can offer some predictive value about where the future of the play may lie and so contribute to production and reception futures. Again, no better subject than *The Playboy.* From its inception, *The Playboy* was energized by those conflicting qualities of the local and the international. It is sufficiently localized and cannot be profitably moved to West Kansas, and yet its creators were J. M. Synge, up to that time a Parisian poet and translator; W. B. Yeats, in fact if not in reputation a London-based poet fond of citing Scandinavian models; and Lady Gregory, that aristocrat in all the best senses of the word. In current usage, one great gap associated with the play and its makers could be described as that between nationalist and globalist conceptions. This gap certainly will be among the hottest cultural, economic, and even military contexts in which the play will be embedded in its future productions. One cosmopolitan dimension in the background of the play Synge wrote is the Boer War context evident in the 'Kharki cut-throats' references and related language. A century later, the context resonates, even though now the resonance is no longer to a British empire. In this way the production history of the play can at least hope to project areas of relevance most likely to resonate in its future.

The history of The Playboy of the Western World in America teaches us several things about the play, some of which complement what we know from its life at home, and some of which add new interest to its performance and potentials in performance. The play has been on the professional stage in America very consistently since 1911. It has been staged in America by visiting Irish companies and by American producing companies. It was first performed professionally in America by an Abbey company touring from New England to Chicago under the title Irish Players. In 1998 it was staged by the Steppenwolf Company in Chicago, one of the most distinguished American theatre companies. From 1911 to 1998 The Playboy of the Western World has been standard repertory fare in America. However, the nature of the productions has changed in important ways. There are three phases of American production and reception of The Playboy, each roughly co-inciding with a third of the twentieth century.

The first phase, beginning with the Irish Players tour in 1911, was as riotous as the debut in Dublin and, given the touring format, had the added distinction of inspiring theatre riots in many places. Recently, Nicholas Grene, Lionel Pilking-ton, Ben Levitas, Christopher Morash and others have written very powerfully about the debut of the play in Dublin in the midst of nationalist debates. In America, the play was similarly seen as a social critique, rather than an artistic statement, and it was denounced in rhetoric about libel familiar from Dublin four years earlier. However, the polarities and positions in America could not be as directly related to Home Rule as they were in Dublin; that context was diminished or entirely absent except as a vehicle for fundraising by Clan na Gael and others. Instead, in America the power of the play to please or to displease as a social critique derived from class distinctions, as in fact theatre disputes in America frequently have been at least since the Astor Place Riot of 1849. Certainly, Irish America did not like to see its place of origin deconstructed so efficiently. But Irish America, and especially Irish Catholic America, re-presented a working class and spent more time, probably much more profitably, organizing for labor than for Home Rule.

On the first Irish Players tour, *The Playboy* was staged on college campuses and in art houses, and not, as in Dublin, in a renovated Mechanics Hall on a familiar stretch of Abbey Street. The class gap between producers of the play and its audiences was particularly prominent in New York City, the home, of course, of American cultural mandarins. In New York, Lady Gregory stayed at the very posh Algonquin Hotel, and much was made of Yeats's British pension. Performances of the play in New York were at the distinctly upscale Maxine Elliott Theatre, established and named for a diva of the American stage who deplored musicals and popular entertainment. The rioters had never been to the Maxine Elliott Theatre before. Lady Gregory took pleasure in naming those arrested by trade: mason, bar-tender, harness-maker, and so forth. In America, the play succeeded in giving affront, but the insult cannot be translated entirely into nationalist positions. So one lesson to be derived from the American experience is the power of the play to ignite onstage and offstage class conflict and dynamic. This is a *Playboy of the Western World* that, in reference to American theatre parallels, played much less like *Oklahoma!* and much more like *Tobacco Road*, another play perceived as libelling a local culture, that of the American south, for the amusement of an urban elite. The reception remained essentially the same when the Abbey sent two additional tours immediately after, though the degree of outrage and the numbers of arrests diminished.

However, in America, by mid-century, the play lost its identity as a social critique and took on a new one as high art. When the Abbey tours returned to America in 1932 after a twenty-year absence, the riots and the power of the play as social critique were generally evoked as ancient history about dead issues. For example, in 1932 Richard Watts, a long-time newspaper critic in New York, explained to readers that 'the Irish, in the manner of oppressed races, were inclined to be sensitive about national honor', that such was no longer the case, and so the play is now:

> one of the definitely great modern comedies: a work so lyric in the beauty of its language and yet so robustly hilarious in its hearty humour that you must go back to Shakespeare to find its peer.

There is nothing particularly wrong with this view of the play, but it should be noted that between the first and the second series of tours the Abbey performances of *The Playboy* have been transformed in American perception from incendiary to poetic. The text certainly didn't change, and the production style remained relatively consistent. In fact, by the tour of 1932, there is already some muttering about the Abbey Players coasting on habitual routines. Nor did the political context wholly change: Roy Foster's biography of Yeats describes in detail Irish-America lobbying Eamon De Valera at this time to remove *The Playboy* from the repertory. Yeats, as producer of the tour, responded that *The Playboy* was now a subject for 'lectures in American universities and schools', a claim, whether true or untrue, that probably would have added to the resolve

Sara Allgood as Pegeen, Barry Fitzgerald as Michael James, and Arthur Shields as Christy Mahon, in a revival of *The Playboy* from the 1920s.

From Christopher Fitz-Simon, The Irish Theatre.

of the play's opponents in America. De Valera, who lost this match to Yeats, argued that *The Playboy* would offend that audience he called the 'Irish exiles'.

However, by the 1930s the Irish in America who had most loudly denounced the play in 1911 had lost interest in it, and the 'Irish exiles' lobbying De Valera were more interested in the domestic politics in Ireland than theatre in America. That left *The Playboy of the Western World* to an artistic audience that in it found art as surely as the political audience found it political. Instead of harness-makers and bartenders, the play was a focus for the writers and readers of journals like *Theatre Arts Monthly*, which, in 1933, extolled Synge's play in these terms:

> The Abbey theatre audiences are bound to feel a keen sympathy for the strange, earthbound, imaginative, inconsistent, delightful thing that is Irish character. And above all, there is the music of their voices, full-toned and mellow, that in the best of their dialect plays produces a feast of sound.

And so where there was political offence one now finds beautiful sound without content. It is quite striking that *The Playboy* would acquire this reputation for 'lyricism', a word that echoes through American reviews, at a time when the American stage was becoming more rather than less political. In the 1930's major Broadway shows began to focus on race or class and large organizations outside New York such as the Federal Theatre Project were advancing populist ideals of participatory democracy.

At mid-century Brooks Atkinson, in that very influential position of drama critic of the *New York Times* for 35 years, set this perception of *The Playboy* in stone. He first wrote about the play in 1932 when the Abbey Theatre resumed touring in America. Mimicking Synge, he wrote:

> For it is a long time surely, as Margaret Flaherty would say, since such poetry talk was spoken in a New York theatre and since voices swung up and down the scale with the flow of Irish rhythms.

He was not stingy in praise: 'when you hear peasants in Synge's comedy transmuting the common events of the day into a troubadour's magic', he wrote of this Abbey production, 'you know what sort of writing the theatre needs to redeem its lost heritage'. This kind of praise, however, was not necessarily what the company or the playwright might have sought. Fourteen years later, in 1946, Atkinson reviewed a largely American production that he thought 'too literal' because the play was a 'lyric masterpiece' and the cast was unable to achieve full performance 'of a play that overflows with spoken music'. And then, twelve years after that, in 1958, he reviewed another American production that also failed to do justice 'to the fresh music of country speech' in the play. Atkinson described the production as antidote to globalized homogenization of language because now 'radio blankets whole countries'. So in mid-century the incendiary play has in America, or at least in New York, become an aesthetic exercise tied to quaintness and to an enviable obsolescence in an increasingly technological world. Surely these are promising contexts for the play now, when media are much more pervasive than radio, and when the relations of what Atkinson called 'remote places' are even more clearly polarization of superpowers and smaller opponents.

It is also worth noting the kind of language that Atkinson and other American reviewers extolled for 'full-toned and mellow' music. The power of the play today seems to reside less in what Pegeen calls 'poets' talk' than in the harder language that predominates in the play and makes the love scenes exceptional. Much more representative of the power of the play are Michael James's less than lyrical lines on 'five men, aye, and six men, stretched out retching speechless on the holy stones'. These lines in Act Three interrupt a love scene and make its swooning optimism – the center, for Atkinson, of lyricism – seem, in context, delusional. Nicholas Grene and others have written on the 'Black Pastoral' quality of *The Playboy*: its introduction of evil and violence into a verdant ideal. The malevolent dimension of the play is what inspired demonstrators against it earlier in the century. Their protests confirmed the powerful combination in the play of the language of violence and suggestions of chaos and slow death. In this Eden, Jimmy Farrell knows 'a party was kicked in the head by a red mare, and he went killing horses a great while, till he eat the insides of a clock and died after' and, in this play, one of the jollier drinking toasts is to:

> the wonders of the western world, the pirates, preachers, poteen-makers, with the jobbing jockies, parching peelers, and the juries fill their stomachs selling judgments of the English law.

In hindsight, 'lyric masterpiece' seems, at best, a partial description.

In addition, there is a downside to being celebrated for soaring lyrical artistic performances of a certain kind associated with 'Irish rhythms'. The liability was described very well by Seamus Deane in reference to Brian Friel. Deane pointed out how that kind of compliment quickly runs its course into a kind of patronizing praise. In his introduction to a selection of Friel's plays, Deane described how in the great Broadway success of *Philadelphia, Here I Come!* Friel was 'being silently exploited' for 'virtuoso performance of the kind of Irish eloquence which had come to be expected from Irish playwrights in particular'. That is, the work was aestheticized and so neutered, which is what happened to *The Playboy of the Western World* in America at mid-century. The historic lesson for future reference of this phase of *The Playboy*'s career in America is about powerful content that should not be aestheticized away.

Of Atkinson's reviews, the first was of an Irish production and the last two were American productions. In fact, the first American production was a student one at the American Conservatory in 1908, three years before the Irish Players visit. There is a history, of course, of Irish touring productions, but a clear pattern of a century of American productions is, that from early to late century, Irish productions are replaced by American ones in a pattern that creates and confirms the American perception of the play. After all, once the social critique is nullified and the character of the play is located in music, why not perform it ourselves? The result is a rather discouraging and chaotic production history that is frequently constructed, as is the wont of the American stage, as a vehicle for the stars. For example, in 1946 a production was built around Burgess Meredith: the souvenir programme featured him in a silk dress suit, cigarette poised thoughtfully – a precursor of *The Playboy* of magazine fame. That same year, 1946, a summer production on Cape Cod was built around Gregory Peck. The notices included this:

> Peck acted a jaunty vagabond who boasts of killing his father in a potato patch, thus symbolizing the Irishman's contempt for authority. Peck's old Cape Cod friends found him simple and friendly despite his Hollywood success, and critics found his acting excellent after he got over his first-night shyness.

Part of the image of the Abbey in America was as a repertory company remarkable for being outside American production conventions, and transfer of artistic control from Irish originators to American adapters seems to have ensured less than extraordinary results.

In 1971, the centenary of Synge's birth was celebrated in New York with a major American production at Lincoln Center. No less than Howard Clurman of Group Theatre fame followed the usual pattern of citing the early riots and praising the music. It also says something about how diffuse the play was getting for Americans that Clurman found that this production made him 'fully understand why Gordon Craig named John Millington Synge his favourite playwright of the Edwardian era'. By way of introduction, Clurman introduced readers of the *Nation* to the play as 'prose which is sheer poetry' and the country of origin as 'a mystic land, peopled by heroes and saints'. Clurman did allow that 'the play's veracity must prove searing', but it is hard to imagine, sixty years after the first Irish Players tour, how he thought this play could offend, since he located its character in 'a wistful, almost sorrowful, remoteness of background, the aching haggardness of the boggy horizon'. This general haze is in sharp contrast to the incendiary point perfectly visible to all involved sixty years before. The 1970's is the period of that musical adaptation *Back Country*, and so in late 20th century *The Playboy of the Western World* could be said to find its parallel from the American stage not in *Oklahoma!*, and not in *Tobacco Road*, but in Meredith Wilson's *The Music Man*, which is a parallel tale of white lies and big talk that has in common with the American *Playboy* of this period a sanitized quality as different from its saucy musical precursors in Rodgers and Hart or Cole Porter as this *Playboy* is different from its violent and politically aggressive earlier productions.

The effect of leaving us to produce our own *Playboys of the Western World* has in my opinion been to render the play incomprehensible, but that has not limited the play's popularity or perceived artistic merit in America. It is offered regularly by the Irish Repertory in New York City. As noted, Douglas Hughes and Steppenwolf Theatre in Chicago, experts at reviving classics in vivid ways, such as *Death of a Salesman* or *Long Day's Journey into Night*, staged a widely admired production in the 1990's.The Los Angeles production also previously mentioned was praised by *Variety* as 'exceptionally strong', a term to be closely analyzed in the context of *Variety* and of Los Angeles, neither of which is particularly consistent with Synge's ideals. That great gap finds wonderful expression in Pegeen's reference in the play to how 'the mad Mulrannies were driven from California and they lost in their wits'.

In New York, Chicago, or California, *The Playboy* produced by Americans is generally conceived as sentimental and exotic, and thus the play becomes entrapped by the kind of patronizing praise identified by Seamus Deane. One question the American history of the play especially emphasizes, then, is this: why is Synge's play not transportable in performance the way that the works of, for example, Dario Fo, Eugene Ionesco, or Tom Stoppard are? Part of the answer has to be the power of the Kiltartan dialect invented for the play and the discouraging transmutations that occur when that language is not handled by professional Kiltartans. But the language alone has not prevented credible and successful American productions of Shaw, Yeats, Friel, McPherson, McDonagh, or McGuinness. Even if Synge's language is granted a greater degree of difficulty, that alone cannot fully explain the particular issue of authenticity surrounding *The Playboy* more than Synge's other plays and his plays more than other Irish ones. The irony of a century of production history that is especially evident in the American record of *The Playboy* is that the realist, documentary, and almost anthropological sense of the play originally communicated in Synge's preface about only using words 'heard among the country people of Ireland' seems to have prevailed after the demise of the political and the lyrical versions of the play. For Americans, *The Playboy* is always exotic, and the failure or at best limitation of American productions is an inability to replicate that exoticism. That, too, is a great gap, one between artists and audiences, and it appears to lend special power to *The Playboy of the Western World*. In the twentieth century vocabulary of import, export, and trade balances, it can be said that to tap this power of Synge's play seems to demand Irish production at the same time that it demands international audience. There are no doubt other powers to be harnessed in internal productions for Irish audiences, where there are a variety of local issues and claims to ownership. But it may be a peculiarly twenty-first century condition of Synge's play that this local vision requires international dissemination for full effect. Perhaps some revelatory power of a similar exteriorization of local vision explains the fate of the Mulrannies driven mad by California.

Finally, there is another lesson of the American history of *Playboy* productions that makes very visible that great gap the text describes as lying between a gallous tale and a dirty deed. For Americans seeking authentic Irish productions, that is the dynamic of performance in all of the new associations of that word. In America, especially, performance of *The Playboy* makes visible the distance between the performers and the audience, a transaction that the play represents in the distance between Christy and the good people of the village. One great power that *The Playboy of the Western World* shares with a number of other great plays is the manner in which the performance onstage, by Christy, for the villagers, mirrors the performance in the theatre, by the cast, for the audience. That quality of theatricality is heightened when an Arthur Shields, for example, is playing Christy in New York, for example, and not Burgess Meredith or Gregory Peck. One likely context for future productions of the play could be the whole conception of performance studies, performativity, and performance as meta-commentary that the play stages. Reconstruction around the integral performative qualities of Christy and his onstage audience could help create productions conceptualized on performance rather than Irish politics, Irish lyricism, or Irish exoticism. The discipline of Performance Studies may be the contribution to the future of *The Playboy of the Western World* that America can make in place of a distinguished history of American productions. That would be, to use a common phrase from that discipline, a 'performance of culture' for a twenty-first century in which John Synge's play continues to move, in one of the play's reiterative phrases, 'from Mayo to the Western world'.

4 | 'Quaint Pastoral Numbskulls': Siobhán McKenna's *Playboy* Film

Adrian Frazier

The *Playboy of the Western World* film starring Siobhán McKenna (1923-86) began as a play on the Gaiety stage on 15 September 1960 in the Dublin Theatre Festival. The show was directed by Shelah Richards (1903-85), an actress in the Abbey from the 1920s, and the first Nora Clithero in *The Plough and the Stars* ... and, by the by, Denis Johnston's wife and Jennifer Johnston's mother.[1] And that is all I shall say about Shelah Richards, for I have a hunch that in this case, the key figures were the producer and the star.

The producer was Brendan Smith (1917-89).[2] In October 1960, Smith, a bald, stocky entrepreneur with a goatee and

---

[1] Shelah Richards also directed Siobhán McKenna in The Playboy of the Western World for the Edinburgh Festival in 1951; see Micheál Ó hAodha, Siobhán: A Memoir of an Actress (Brandon: Dingle, Co. Kerry, 1994), 44.

[2] Born in Essex, Brendan Smith founded the Brendan Smith Theatre Academy with his wife Beryl Fagan in 1943; became Chair of the Board of the Olympia Theatre;started the Dublin Theatre Festival in 1957 with funds from Bord Fáilte; and with Lord Killanin co-produced the film of *The Playboy of the Western World* in 1961. See obituary by Ossie Trilling, *Irish Independent*, (4 December 1989), p.12.

winning smile, took the production to festivals in Berlin and Venice, before settling in for a four-month engagement at the Piccadilly Theatre, London. [3] What he had to sell was an Irish star with an international reputation, Siobhán McKenna. In a fit of Celto-mania, the *Times* reviewer hailed Siobhán McKenna as the very image of Gráinne and Deirdre, 'elfin-eyed', with 'high Slavic cheekbones', and 'scarlet hair tumbling to the waist' – hair that is scarlet![4] She was, he imagined, 'the ideal of Celtic woman-hood', or at least 'close to' it.

The advance publicity made much of the new way in which Synge's words would be spoken. The speech sounds made by the Irish actors would sometimes be, according to the pre-performance article in *The Times*, 'outside the range of the English phonetic system', and thus probably impossible for Londoners to follow. This accent was taken, the newspaper explained, directly from 'Connacht Gaelic', the original source from which Synge's dialogue was itself a 'deviation'.[5] The actors, unlike Synge, were natives, so this 'Connacht Gaelic' would be uttered in an unforced, natural way.

But there is no evidence that anyone in the cast for this *Playboy* was actually born west of the Shannon. One was from Bradford, one from Navan, and two from Belfast; the place of

---

[3] 'Irish Actors to Tour Europe', *The Times*, 5 September 1961, p.15. Email from Lelia Doolan, 10 Jan 2004, regarding the Shelah Richards production that toured Germany: 'Just spoke to Jennifer [Johnston] and she'll come later in the week and could stay over for your round-table. Can talk about her mother's [Shelah Richards'] Dublin Theatre Festival production which we did sometime around 1960, toured to the Continent and then played for a few months in London. I played Sara Tansey in that – as well as other parts in a couple of productions of *The Heart's A Wonder* – in Dublin, London (and Mullingar!). And of course, there's the Brecht production in the Berliner Ensemble in the mid-fifties which I'd seen there as a student and which we visited again during the tour with Shelah R's production (Siobhán as Pegeen and Donal Donnelly as Christy) when we were playing in the Hebbel in West Berlin.'

[4] 'Pegeen Mike's Play', *The Times,* 16 September 1960, p.16.

[5] 'Strong Acting in *The Playboy*', *The Times*, 13 October 1960, p.18.

birth for the others is unknown to me.[6] Thus, the point about accent was ideological, not factual. Not just were the Irish going to make no concession to BBC English, they were ostensibly going to musicalize Hiberno-English, so that it would arise from citizens of the Irish Republic, not from Synge. The whole production would be Celtic, ideal, Gaelic, pure, native, and, of course, completely authentic, 'to the manner born', according to the publicity, as if speaking of dukes and duchesses in their manor homes, not Belmullet tenants in famine cottages. But sure, nearly all the Irish were descended from kings and queens of times gone by, weren't they? Brendan Smith – himself born in Essex – excelled at getting Bord Failte money for his theatre projects, and for his film, he aimed to restyle Synge's play for de Valera's Ireland. It was to be a tourism poster for Shannon airport and development on the western seaboard.[7]

After the London run, but before filming began in the summer of 1961, the play moved to Siobhán McKenna's birthplace, Belfast, and the Empire Theatre. But one night's performance – that of May 10 – had to be called off. Pegeen Mike was needed elsewhere, though it was not in the Tir-na-nogue of Celtic queens. MGM had to reshoot a few scenes for its latest New Testament epic, *The King of Kings*, and the Virgin Mary – a.k.a. Siobhán McKenna – was required on set in London.

The Hollywood company, attempting to capitalize on the success of *Ben Hur* (1959), had found a perfectly Aryan Jesus in Jeffrey Hunter, a blue-eyed blond hunk, previously featured in support of John Wayne in cowboy movies like *The Searchers*. Once they had shaved his armpits for the Crucifixion, he was just right for the part of Jesus. For the Blessed Virgin Mary there was no place for casting agents to turn except to Catholic Ireland, and Siobhán McKenna.

---

[6] Donal Donnelly, who played Christy, was from Bradford; John Cowley, who played Michael James, was from Navan; and Eithne Dunne (Widow Quin) and Siobhán McKenna (Pegeen Mike) were both from Belfast.

[7] Shannon Airport became a compulsory port-of-call for flights from the USA in February 1945 and a duty-free zone in 1947.

Siobhán McKenna as the Virgin Mary in 'The King of Kings'

Jeffrey Hunter as Jesus in 'The King of Kings'

For the week of 10 September 1956, she had made the cover of *Life* magazine for her holy and impassioned St. Joan. In that role, she had been both ardently Catholic and ardently anti-British in her republicanism. As mother of our Lord, she became doubly sainted…no, infinitely so.

However, could Siobhán McKenna trail all the glories of these past roles – republican saint, saga queen, Blessed Virgin Mary, and Irish speaker to the manner born – into the part of a Mayo barmaid, 'a girl you'd see itching and scratching, and she

Siobhán McKenna as St. Joan

Life Magazine, *10 September 1956*

with a stale stink of poteen on her from selling in the shop'?[8] The playtext was no bar to Siobhán McKenna, the brilliant daughter of a Belfast-born UCG Math professor, educated in a Monaghan convent. She could, and did, do all that – especially in the film version that began shooting a month after the Belfast run of *The Playboy* concluded.

The location used for the film was not Gaoth Sáile on the Erris penisula in County Mayo, original setting for the play, though that is certainly a very eerie and beautiful place. It still has a feel of vast emptiness with the sea on one side and distant mountains far across a bog on the other. No, only the most

[8] J.M. Synge, *Collected Works*, ed. Ann Saddlemyer, vol.4 (Colin Smythe: Gerrard's Cross, Buck.; Catholic University of America Press, 1982), p.127.

stupendously cinematic seascape was acceptable, and that was Inch Strand, in County Kerry, far more accessible to Shannon Airport, and so inevitably picture-perfect that David Lean would use the Kerry coastline again in *Ryan's Daughter* [1970].

Brendan Smith brought on board as co-producers Daniel O'Donnell and Michael, Lord Killanin (1914-1999), to form 'The Four Provinces Film Company'. Killanin had worked with Laurence Olivier on *Henry V* (1944, filmed in Co. Wicklow) and with John Ford on *The Quiet Man* (1952, filmed in Co. Galway). The producers secured funding from Bord Fáilte, hired a director at the end of an undistinguished but Irish career, Brian Desmond Hurst (1900-1986), and a cinematographer at the beginning of his own quite spectacular career, Geoffrey Unsworth. He would be the cameraman for *2001: A Space Odyssey* in 1968 and *Superman* in 1978. In Unsworth's Eastman Kodak photography, the first image of Pegeen Mike's bodice is so brightly red around its line of twenty liquorice-drop buttons that one nearly has to squint. Just as pure a tint is the white of Shawn Keogh of Killakeen's flannel collarless jacket, the authentic *báinín* worn by the western islanders, laundered apparently by the film crew through three cycles in some fierce, 1950s American detergents.

Siobhán McKenna as Pegeen Mike

Production head Bill Lang arrived at Inch July 1961 with a crew of eighty, including actors and technicians. It was boom time for Kerry. Fifty thousand pounds were spent locally in food bills, lodgings, car hire, and wages for stand-ins, security-men, extras for crowd scenes (from six traveller families), gofers, boatmen, jockeys, dancers, and musicians.[9]

The film, it had best be admitted straightaway, though I suppose it has already been strongly implied, is very bad, both as a film, and as a version of *The Playboy*. Its general shortcoming as a film is that too little was done to turn the stage play into something for the screen. Outside of significant cuts to the playtext – of which more later – the dialogue in the film is that of the play, and, for a film, there is too much talk and too little of anything else. In addition, the actors behave as if they are on a stage, and the cameraman behaves as if he's in the front row of the audience, but rising up and down in his seat, or leaning this way and that, to get a better view of the action. Whenever there is a large group on stage, excuse me, *on set*, they arrange themselves into a tableau, then shift quickly to another tableau, always forming a semi-circle or angled line facing the imaginary auditorium. In fast forward on video, the mechanics of the blocking is comically, cruelly apparent.

For instance, in Act Two, Sara Tansey has fetched from behind the bar a bottle of whiskey, and for theatrical reasons she is standing with the two other village girls behind the bench on which Christy sits with the Widow Quin. Sarah Tansey pours the pair a lovers' toast, drunk at once by the two with inter-linked arms. Suddenly, Pegeen Mike comes in at the door. Arms unlink, glasses are set down, the tableau dissolves. Not a step lost, the actors swiftly take up new positions and hold them through the next speeches. On one side are the three girls ranged in an angled row beside the door with Widow Quin. On the other side stands Pegeen Mike, while Christy scrunches up cowering beside the hearth. The actors move in drill in this fashion throughout the play, like soldiers on parade. It's absurd.

Another incomplete translation of play to film results in an absurdity when Christy goes outside to wash his face in the

---

[9] According to an article in *The Kerryman* (19 August 1961), the 'shoestring' £130,000 budget for the film required many to work at half their usual fees. Siobhán McKenna, it was said, received between five and ten thousand pounds for her part.

morning – aha! An exterior shot with Inch strand in the background, to the delight of cameraman Geoffrey Unsworth. Facing into the camera, Christy loudly speaks out his soliloquy at the opening of Act Two. Is he mad? the film-watcher wonders.

On the other hand, the film is a not just a bad film but a very bad version of the play too because, paradoxically, it is too little the play itself…either not enough *a* film, or not enough *the* play. Indeed, *The Playboy* film is in full flight from the force of Synge's play. Sometimes this evasiveness about a still troublesome classic becomes apparent in the cuts. Many are made in the scene of the guessing-game in Act One when the townspeople try to figure out for what crime the newcomer is wanted. While Synge may have been having the characters simply citing cases at the Mayo Assizes of the 1890s, and Mayo was then crime-ridden compared with counties in the Pale, the impression is given by his selection of crimes that the people thereabouts are exceptionally ingenious in the ways they break the law. At any rate, they are as avidly interested in outlandish villainy as today's readers of *The Sun*. The producers of the cinematic *Playboy*, however, had no time for the mention of crimes other than stealing or violence against bailiffs, agents, or landlords, in other words, all 'justifiable' crimes of liberation from an unjust feudal system. That anyone in Ireland coined false money or took two wives is not admitted by the film. The 'mad Mulrannies [that] were driven from California and they lost their wits' is no great loss, and perhaps lawyers in Los Angeles would have found grounds for a lawsuit there.[10] And even the cancellation of the joke equating 'Dan Davie's Circus and holy missioners of the North' shows a surprising sensitivity to Ulster Protestants.[11] But a worry emerges that the producers were chauvinistically more concerned about the sensitivities of the post-colonial Irish than those of other people.

---

[10] Synge, *Collected Plays*, vol. 2, p.59.
[11] ibid., p.71.

The worst cut, however, is the complete elimination of the first half of Act Three, everything after the sports on the strand up to the love-scene between Christy and Pegeen. Thus, there is no gallows humour between Jimmy and Philly about the bodies buried in bogs, no reappearance of Old Mahon trying – just like his son – to impress strangers with the tale of what was done to him, no admission by Old Mahon that he likes to drink himself paralytic with the girls of Limerick and was once strait-jacketed in an asylum – so prostitution, rural alcoholism, and schizophrenia are erased; no declaration of amazement – 'Good rider! He's through it again!' – by the father at what his own son has achieved in the pony races;[12] no plot on the part of Philly to stage a rematch between Old Mahon and Christy for the sake of the sport that will be in it, even should murder this time truly come to pass.

Instead of all this, we get an elaborate but at the same time rushed sequence of tableaux of the sports on Inch strand, all unaccompanied by dialogue – rather weird after every other frame in the picture had been dictated by the dialogue. Curraghs rising and falling on vast waves come spectacularly ashore and are dragged up high on the beach. Jockeys for ponies appear, decked out in striped polo jerseys. A crowd gathered from a half a dozen traveller families, camped in caravans in a lay-by near Inch, assemble to watch the pony race.[13] The art consultant for the film was painter Patrick Scott, and he self-consciously recreated in Technicolor a number of Jack Yeats paintings in this part of the film. It's like *tableaux vivants* of classics from the National Gallery. The racing is followed by a game of throwing sticks at a man in a barrel (Christy hits him the second time he puts up his head). Next comes boxing in a raised ring built on the strand. After two or three blows are exchanged – neither combatant bothers to put up his dukes – Christy decks his larger opponent with a haymaker, and raises his fists in triumph. The ring is rapidly

---

[12] ibid., p.141.

[13] 'Tinkers Head For Inch and the 'Great Money',' *Kerryman* (29 July 1961).

cleared for set dancing by the 'Tralee Dancers', forerunners of Siamsa Tíre, in which Christy is paired with a neatly stepping Pegeen, as Shawn Keogh of Killakeen watches defeatedly, and Paddy Moloney and future members of the Chieftains provide the diddle-de-dee music.[14]

The step-dancing after the sports on the strand

The music dies, with still no sight of Old Mahon. Christy then leads Pegeen Mike away into the sawgrass on the dunes for their love scene.

Siobhán McKenna was very pleased with how, the wind blowing in the grasses, waves heard in the distance, this outdoor scene went.[15] I wasn't. But I have yet to see a pro-

[14] The Tralee dancers are pictured in the 12 August 1961 *Kerryman*, on their way to the 10 August shooting of the fair scene, p.1.

[15] Ó hAodha, *Siobhán*, 93. According to a reporter for the Kerryman, the love scene was played in grasses that proved, even if picturesque, particularly prickly. Nuala O'Sullivan, a 'lass from Dingle', and Killarney man Pat Tobin, both stand-ins, were used for the set-ups, so that the stars had to endure only brief periods prostrate in the

duction that reveals what I see in the text. Synge was not just shocked but physically stirred by the bodily freedom and flirtatiousness of the girls on Aran and the western counties: they would sit on his knee, tickle and tease him.[16] At the time of writing *The Playboy*, he was carrying on a love affair with a pretty young girl in the Abbey troupe, Molly Allgood, and she was not at all shy around men. He then cast her as Pegeen. The part is that of a barmaid who is more than a practiced flirt; she is a previously frustrated romantic, the kind that would give all for love. I mention these facts because I think that Synge saw, and the play dramatizes, a western people that were both violent and, surprisingly, highly sexed – at least compared to the Protestants of Victorian Dublin. The Widow Quin, remember, is the classic lusty young widow of literature and life, but in the film the role is taken by a large Scottish actress with a heavy low bosom, 50-year-old Elspeth March; she had been playing the role since 1938.[17] She looks more like a mother to the 26-year-old Welsh actor playing Christy, Gary Raymond, than an attractive proposition. As a result, Pegeen's jealousy seems superficial and silly; no love triangle exists.

---

sawgrass.' The whole thing is exciting', Miss O'Sullivan said (*Kerryman*, 29 July 1961).

[16] J. M. Synge, 'The Aran Islands', *Collected Works*, v. 2, *Prose* (Oxford UP: London, 1966): 'the strange beauty of the women', p.54; an Aran woman nursing another's baby wore 'a curiously whimsical expression', p.70; 'the women and girls, when they had no men with them, usually tried to make fun with me', p.83; 'Is it tired you are, stranger', said one girl. 'Bedad, it is not, little girl', I answered in Gaelic, "it is lonely I am"', p.83; 'a beautiful young woman I had spoken to a few times last year slipped in, and after a wonderfully simple and cordial speech of welcome, she sat down on the floor beside me...The complete absence of shyness or self-consciousness in most of these people gives them a peculiar charm, and when this young woman leaned across my knees to look nearer at some photograph that pleased her, I felt more than ever the strange simplicity of island life', p.106.

[17] *Irish Press* (19 March 1961), p.3. Elspeth March was an understudy to Maire O'Neill in the role in the late 1930s, and first played it in 1938.

The text is insistent about the physical passion of the lovers. Christy talks of himself and Pegeen making 'mighty kisses with our wetted mouths', but even contemporary productions often omit to indicate any sort of sex appeal in either Christy or Pegeen, much less the Widow Quin.[18]

A good thing about the love-scene in the film is that they take it lying down, with Pegeen at one moment 'stretched back unto [her] necklace in the flowers of the earth'. [19]

Pegeen and Christy: The love scene on the beach

Lying side by side, of course, not one on top of the other. And Christy doesn't get, as the text promises he will, his 'two hands stretched around [her]' nor does he 'squeez[e] kisses on her puckered lips'.[20] He says, 'Feel my two hands around you', but she can't possibly do so, because at the time the pair are sitting side by side and his hands are either plunged in the sand or

[18] Synge, vol. 2, p.149.
[19] ibid.
[20] ibid., p.147.

gesticulating in the air. When she then lies back in the grass, her eyes are cast piously to the sky; she does not look into his eyes. Finally, she sits up and leans into him, and a light brush of a kiss is enacted, from which the two withdraw in religious wonder. He tries to get another, but she doesn't let him have it – she hears her father coming from the wake, just in time to save the day. At any rate, no great loss to the voyeur. Christy was played by Gary Raymond, a handsome, lanky Welshman then 24, and Siobhán McKenna was a chunky 37, so it was a bit like Christy was scheming to get a sexual introduction from his auntie.

Further disappointments follow at the play's climax. Christy does not actually put on the dress the girls bring him as a disguise; so no allusion is made to Heracles among the Amazons. Pegeen does not burn his leg with a hot ember, thus one more blemish is removed from the 'ideal of Celtic womanhood', and one more spike of irony from the playtext.

None of these excisions and euphemistic interpretations, however, matches in terms of cowardice the deliberately evasive playing style of the whole company. Since the production does not accept that Synge's play is what it is, and since it can neither cut everything, nor write new scenes that are better, it must play those scenes that exist on paper as if they made no sense at all. As a result, everyone in the play puts on a face of hyper-naïve, wondering innocence, like so many simpletons. Kenneth Tynan had picked this up in the London production. He could not, Tynan wrote, 'devote my full attention to a play in which all the characters are numbskulls – and quaint pastoral numbskulls at that'.[21]

Tynan, however, makes a serious mistake. He attributes the fault to the playwright, not to the actors. Synge valued the 'reality' and 'joy' of the people of the Erris Penisula, joy even in the years following their 1898 famine. He saw something 'superb and wild' in them that he wished to transfer to the

---

[21] Ó hAodha, *Siobhán*, p.68.

stage.[22] But the reality of those people was too much for the cinematic version of an Irish classic backed by Bord Fáilte, a semi-state body. Things the author saw as vital virtues the producers saw as sins or defects of nature; things the author saw as defects, the producers saw as innocence or even positive virtues. Better, anyway, that the Irish of the pristine west were idiots, watched over by Father Reilly, than that they were, as Synge wrote them, violent, sexy, and wild.

At the beginning of this talk, it was hypothesized that the star and the producer of the *Playboy* movie were responsible for the way it turned out, and the director of the stage version, Shelah Richards, was not. But I do not wish to hold a single actress accountable for its failures, certainly not at a conference held in the city where her career began and in the theatre where she played her last great role. No, I won't blame her, not even if the film in huge, red Celtic script gives Siobhán McKenna top billing, ahead of the title of the play.

Siobhán McKenna is only the star, and a star embodies the imagination of others, sometimes of an author, sometimes a producer or director, and sometimes – as I think in this case – of a whole people. The publicity about the re-Gaelicization of Synge's dialogue through the actor's voices clearly reflects a period when Eamon de Valera could tell an after-Mass meeting that:

> The Irish language is the bond that…enabled [our] people to resist all efforts to make them English. It would be useful to us today, when we have poured in upon us from every direction, influences which are contrary to the traditional views of our people…[T]he character [of our people] consist of very simple things: earnestness in our work, honesty, and truthfulness.[23]

Siobhán McKenna's picture-house Pegeen materializes right out of de Valera's 'Ireland We Dreamed Of', with comely

---

[22] Synge, pp.53-54.

[23] Quoted, Fintan O'Toole, *The Lie of the Land* (New Island Books: Dublin, 1998), p.85.

maidens step-dancing at the cross-roads. [24] She is also the charming colleen in the fantasy Ireland of JFK's speeches during his June 1963 visit to Galway – an 'Old Ireland that is Old Ireland still', a 'green and misty isle' of faith and fortitude.[25] If she was not the real, this Pegeen was the fantasy Irish woman of the 1950s and 60s.

Of course, now even the real Ireland of July 1961 seems a fantasy, so completely has it disappeared. [26] It was the summer just before the Common Market was formed; just before the first Irish television broadcast. On July 3rd, two weeks before filming started in Kerry, the front-page story was that 10,000 people gathered below Slane Castle. It was not, however, for a rock concert by U2. Well-dressed and lined up in straight rows on the hillside, the ten thousand gazed at a spot between two trees, where Mass was being celebrated on the very spot that St. Patrick kindled the Paschal fire in 433, establishing Christianity in Ireland. On July 8th, the *Irish Press* ran the following massive headlines: 'PERIL TO YOUTH, Pope Warns on Immoral Films, TV'. A week later, another bulletin from the Vatican was the lead story: 'FIGHT HUNGER', a papal imperative qualified in the subheading, 'Private Property a Right'. While the film was being shot, the results of the most recent census were published: the population of Ireland had fallen by 2.9%, and was at its lowest recorded number. It becomes harder every day to recall what life in Ireland was like a few decades ago.

There was one very good thing about Siobhán McKenna's performance as Pegeen in the film. It created a setting for her explosive 'Mommo' in *Bailegangaire* (Druid Theatre, 1985), a play which splendidly desecrates 'the Ireland [de Valera] dreamed of'. Author Tom Murphy and director Garry Hynes drew out of the Irish star a sense of buried tribal realities, ones that exploded many myths about innocence, ould Ireland, and comely

---

[24] Maurice Moynihan, ed., *Speeches and Statements by Eamon de Valera 1917-73* (Gill and Macmillan: Dublin; St. Martin's, NY: 1980), 466.

[25] O'Toole, p.51.

[26] The film was quickly shot between 18 July and 19 August 1961 (information from reports in the *Irish Press*).

maidens. Indeed, to stretch things in order to make a point, *Bailegangaire* is a rendition of *The Playboy* – its volatile cocktail of laughter and violence, loneliness and storytelling – that is more accurate than the Bord Fáilte movie, though not a single line of Synge's script is uttered in it.

5 | Two London Playboys: Before and After Druid

Nicholas Grene

In August 1999 there was an occasion on Inis Meáin to celebrate the opening of Teach Synge, the house of the McDonagh family where Synge had stayed on his visits to Aran, which has been refurbished by its owner Treasa Ní Fhatharta. Among the notables who flew over for the event were Stephen Rea and Brid Brennan. As these actors had been a famous Christy Mahon and Pegeen Mike in their day, they were asked to read extracts from the play together in front of the cottage. It was a time-warp moment to hear them acting out Christy and Pegeen's love-duet. But listening to their lines brought home to me the different times, different productions that were being summoned back: it was 1975 meeting 1982 in 1999. Rea had been the Christy in a spectacularly successful National Theatre production in London directed by Bill Bryden, which played in the company's repertoire from October 1975 to March 1977. Brennan had led as Pegeen in Garry Hynes's landmark 1982 Druid version that had gone on to be revived repeatedly with international tours through the 1980s. I thought I could hear differences between the two: Rea's Christy, more full-throatedly lyrical, with much less variation in rhythm and tone, Brennan as Pegeen speaking with greater modulation of voice and feeling. Anyway, that was one starting point for this paper: I thought I would look at the contrast in styles between the 1975 National

Playboy and the 1980s Druid production. And in so far as that Druid production has come to be seen as shifting later views of the play, I decided to go on to a later revival at the National, directed by Fiona Buffini in 2001, to see what if anything might have changed.

In December 1975, Jeananne Crowley who was playing one of the hero-worshipping girls in the National production published an article in *The Irish Times* headlines 'Requiem for the "Playboy" ':

> It started dramatically: the curtain fell on the opening night of the National Theatre's production of *The Playboy of the Western World* precisely at 9.30 p.m. … At 9.30 precisely, too, a bomb blew up a restaurant in Mayfair.

She went on:

> Since the opening a month ago, and much to the National's surprise, 'Playboy' has had packed houses; although the show has been playing during a wave of massive anti-Irish feeling fuelled by the continued backdrop of kidnapping, bombing, robbery, and now direct assassination all attributed whether correctly or not, to the I.R.A.
>
> Is the attendance a desperate attempt on the part of a bewildered British public to understand the Irish psyche? Or to have their worst fears confirmed?[1]

It is indeed a puzzling question. This was one of the worst times in Anglo-Irish relations, with the violence of the Northern Irish political situation brought home to Londoners as never before. The bomb blast at the Trattoria 'Fiori' in Mayfair on 29 October, the opening night of *Playboy*, had been the second within a week; the previous one, a bomb placed under the car of the M.P. Hugh Fraser killed one of his neighbours. The kidnapping Crowley refers to was that of the Dutch businessman Tiede Herrema, who was finally released on 7 November; the assassination she mentions was of Ross McWhirter killed on his own doorstep on 28 November. And

[1] Jeananne Crowley, 'Requiem for the "Playboy" ', *The Irish Times*, 9 December 1975.

before *The Playboy* had finished its run, there came one of the most notorious events of the time, the murder of Christopher Ewart-Biggs, the British Ambassador to Ireland, in July 1976. What in the style and effect of the National *Playboy* allowed Londoners to watch with enthusiasm this imagined violent Ireland on stage, while outside the theatre violent Irish people were killing their fellow citizens?

The critics were certainly aware of the uncomfortable connections between the play and the extra-theatrical events. Milton Shulman began his *Evening Standard* review with a bitter allusion to IRA sympathizers:

> No doubt the pubs in Dublin, Belfast and Kilburn will soon, if they aren't already, be echoing to songs and poems extolling the deeds of the bombers and kidnappers and murderers in the current Irish troubles.

However, he went on to exempt the play from complicity in such feelings: 'Synge's flood of good humour ... takes the sting out of this callous tale and converts it into one of the most heart-warming comedies of the century'.[2] B.A. Young, the *Financial Times* reviewer, could also see the relevance of the play: 'the casual attitude to life and death, the glorification of the criminal because he has got away with his crime – we see these things reported every day in the Press, and then they are not for laughter'. 'Well', he continued, '*The Playboy* is for laughter anyway, for laughter and pathos and poetry and sympathy, and I doubt if there is a happier evening to be had in the London theatre anywhere at this moment.'[3] The reviews suggest that what made the National *Playboy* such a happy night out was precisely that here was an Ireland without danger.

'Laughter, pathos, poetry, sympathy'; these were the constituent elements. The laughs were certainly there in plenty. Listening to the audio tape in the British Library, which is the

---

2 Milton Shulman, 'The ultimate aphrodisiac', *Evening Standard*, 30 October 1975.

3 B.A. Young, 'The Playboy of the Western World', Financial Times, 30 October 1975.

only extant record of the live production, I was struck by the constant flow of laughter. The actors were not milking them, but they regularly built towards them. Christy's confession – 'Is it killed your father?', 'With the help of God I did surely.' – his first act closing line – 'wasn't I a foolish fellow not to kill my father in the years gone by?' – his set-piece narration of the murder in Act Two, all elicited swelling waves of laughter. The reappearance of Old Mahon in the last scene – 'Are you coming to be killed a third time…?' – produced huge laughs and applause. The audience was clearly having a very good time.

Jeananne Crowley thought the laughter confirmed the audience in their view of the 'paradoxical, whimsical behaviour they expect of the Irish'. That may well be right, and some of the incidental laugh lines suggest that they picked up on other stereotypical images of the Irishman: Christy on the site of the murder – 'Wasn't I digging spuds in the field?' – his anticipation of the easy life of a potboy, with 'never a day's work', both elicited laughs. But the production also drew on associations of Ireland with carnivalesque energies. One reviewer referred to the music that introduced the play as 'the Chieftains' barbaric reel'. At this distance in time it sounds pretty folksy and quaint rather than barbaric. Stills of Christy chaired shoulder-high by the crowd on to the stage after his triumph in the sports, accompanied by live musicians, bring out the intended festive céilidh atmosphere.

Several reviewers stressed the restrained style of the show: as Irving Wardle put it, 'the one decision that runs through every part of the production, set, music and performances, is the refusal to perform the usual nosedive into Syngean lyricism'.[4] 'There is an art nouveau lushness about the language which can seem inflated and over-literary', commented John Barber; 'Mr Bryden keeps it carefully in hand'.[5] In point of fact, Bryden actually lushed up the lyricism in places, splicing in extra lines

[4] Irving Wardle, 'Synge released', *The Times*, 15 October 1976.

[5] John Barber, 'Enthralling 'Playboy' with strong acting', *Daily Telegraph*, 30 October 1975.

Stephen Rea as Christy, chaired round the set in the 1975 National Theatre production directed by Bill Bryden

Photograph by John Haynes

from discarded Synge drafts. So, for instance, in the scene of the girls' first entrance in Act Two, Nelly was given the line, 'Oh, isn't Pegeen a lucky girl to have passed the whole night talking with the like of him?' To which Rhynagh O'Grady, playing Susan, had to take a deep breath and reply:

> She is then. And I'd think little to put a bag on my back and go walking the flinty ways of the world till I'd set my eyes on the like of him, for he should have great height I'm thinking and a fine leg on him, and a smile would knock a lep out of St. Martin's moon.[6]

Synge had the sense to cut lines like this; Bryden put them back in.

---

[6] J.M. Synge, *Collected Works*, IV: *Plays, Book 2*, ed. Ann Saddlemyer (London: Oxford University Press, 1968), p.96.

Both Stephen Rea and Susan Fleetwood won warm praise for their performances as Christy and Pegeen. For Rea at 28 it was a career breakthrough, his first really major London part. I remember myself, seeing the production when it had transferred to the Olivier in the new South Bank National Theatre complex – it actually opened when the company was still in the Old Vic – how impressed I was by the way Fleetwod used her height and presence, how the skinny, hangdog Rea gradually expanded into his hero's role. They were terrific performances. But they were played for sympathy and for charm: the pathos of Christy's loneliness, the warm vulnerability of Pegeen beneath the tartar persona. Charles Lewsen's review in *The Times* was defiantly headed 'A sentimentalist's night of joy':

> There are nights when the stage breaks its banks, unleashing a torrent of pathos and joy. Such it was for me last night as Bill Bryden's production of Synge's intoxicating play now held us in rapt silence, now caused us to laugh from our guts.[7]

The protracted wordless opening of Garry Hynes's Druid production set the tone and couldn't have been less like that of Bill Bryden. Where Fleetwood's Pegeen was discovered 'lying barefoot before the fire at curtain-rise' spelling out 'an order for bridal clothes with the languorous longing of a self-appointed fairy princess',[8] Brennan took long minutes schlepping around the shebeen, finishing her housework, finding pen and paper, replacing the first nib that broke, then writing out each word of the letter with the slow self-consciousness of the barely literate. This was convincingly the Pegeen of Widow Quin's later description, 'a girl you'd see itching and scratching and she with a stale smell of poteen on her from selling in the shop'. If you couldn't smell the poteen, you could see Brid Brennan interrupt her letter-writing to scratch. The keynote of Hynes's production was dirty realism, in the set as in the costuming and perform-

---

7 Charles Lewsen, 'A sentimentalist's night of joy', *The Times*, 30 October 1975.

8 Robert Cushman, 'Down in the country', *The Observer*, 2 November 1975.

ances. Where for the National, Geoffrey Scott had designed 'a white-walled, jug-cluttered, faintly Lorcaesque peasant cottage'[9], the Druid pub was authentic period grunge. The prominently displayed image of the Sacred Heart over the fireplace was notably dilapidated and matched by an equally prominent advertisement for Wills' Gold Flake.

Marie Mullen as the Widow Quin, with King Edward VII's face on Gold Flake advertisement in background; *Playboy of the Western World*, Druid Theatre, 1982.

Courtesy Druid Theatre Company

In the Channel Four broadcast version of the stage production (on which I am largely relying here), there was an ironic fade from the Edward VII face on the poster to the upturned eyes

[9] 'Playboy of the Western World', The Guardian, 30 October 1975.

of the Christ. The lip-service Catholicism of these Mayoites was already embedded in modern materialism; a small St Brigid's cross over the entrance door hinted discreetly at the pagan underpinnings of the culture.

This audience in Galway hardly needs to be instructed in the iconoclastic impact of the 1980s Druid *Playboy*. Setting her face against the quaint and the picturesque, Hynes gave to the play a new grotesquerie and a new violence. Marie Mullen was not the conventionally witchy/sexy Widow Quin, but with her convincingly discoloured teeth and shrewdly calculating face, an altogether tougher character; the hero-worshipping girls, Bairbre ni Chaoimh, Pauline McLynn and Joan Sheehy, cannot have owned a hairbrush between the three of them. Mick Lally as Old Mahon erupting into the tiny shebeen space, with blackened bandage on his head, his face covered in the streaks of dried blood, was a monstrous figure of aggression. But the realization of the violence caused some problems for the production in the final act. The vividly choreographed fight between Christy and his father, the struggles of the lynch-scene, had to be suspended in tableau while Maeliosa Stafford pantingly spoke out Christy's long and elaborate speeches. The difficulty is suggestive of the central dilemma facing the director of the play, the balance to be struck between the realizing impulse and the highly stylized substance of the play's dialogue.

Stage realism is always a shifting term, indicating a perceived style somewhere to the natural side of the theatrical conventions currently in use. So, the 1975 critics (with memories of Siobhán McKenna from fifteen years before) praised the lack of artificiality of the Bryden production, while the much more radical challenges to tradition by Garry Hynes made the National version look conventional by contrast. Fiona Buffini's direction in 2001 clearly built on the style Hynes had established. Derbhle Crotty as Pegeen, like Brid Brennan before, took a protracted time over settling to her letter.

She not only scratched herself; the inclusion of a 'fine-toothed comb' in her order to Seamus Mulroy was prompted by the dis-covery of a nit in her hair. It was not only the opening business that was protracted; the tempo throughout was markedly slower. This was very much a minor key *Playboy*, with

Derbhle Crotty as Pegeen Mike, 2001

very few of the laughs raised by its 1975 National predecessor. The music composed by Conor Linehan, played live in the theatre on guitar, cello and flute, was sombre and atmospheric, a very long way from the sportiveness of the Chieftains.

Buffini attempted also a new sort of social and psychological realism. Pegeen, long-term mistress of the shebeen, wielded a conscious and sure authority. 'You're one of the tinkers, young fellow, is beyond camped in the glen?', she asked in response to Christy's opening request for a glass of porter, looking to place the new customer. 'I am not', said an offended Patrick O'Kane, producing his money by way of rebutting the charge. When this Pegeen sent Widow Quin packing in the second act, it was not in anger but in contemptuous dismissal of her demand for a 'pennyworth of starch'. She and the Widow were evidently old sparring partners; she had the Widow's linen or lack of it well counted.

Both Pegeen and Christy, in this production, were deeply alienated individuals. O'Kane made Christy's misery at first entrance fully felt; he sat by the fire, his back to the company, groaning to himself. Even when questioned about his deed, he never turned to face them until the climactic confession, uttered with real horror. Pegeen, listless and apathetic in the opening scenes, was only gradually aroused out of her near depression by Christy's intense infatuation with herself. She was capable of icy cruelty in the quarrel-scene: there was sadistic emphasis in her imagination of him hanging, 'in great anguish getting your death'. The breakthough in that scene came with Christy's profoundly felt declaration 'I was lonesome all times and born lonesome, I'm thinking, as the moon of dawn', an exposed vulnerability to which Pegeen responded with a sense of affinity. In a production where the romance was always tentative and physical contact between the two was kept to a minimum, it was ironically only when Christy was stretched on the floor under the impact of Old Mahon's violent entrance in Act Three that Pegeen threw herself bodily on top of him in an effort to save him. Shattered by her disillusionment with Christy, genuinely shocked at the apparent second murder, she joined half-heartedly in the lynch-scene. Where Christy's exit speech is traditionally played as a triumphant assertion of self-confidence to the assembled company, in this production it ended with a farewell directed specifically at Pegeen 'from this hour to the dawning of the judgement day'. It was this that prompted the extremity with which Crotty took the famous final lines. As she hit Shawn his box in the ear, she was convulsed with an almost retching grief. The concluding line itself was torn from her in the midst of sobs that continued on in a final fade into darkness. Leaving Pegeen moaning by the fire in exactly the same posture as Christy when he first came in was a way of playing *The Playboy* as a tragedy of lost opportunity for both of them.

The Buffini production had realizing stylistic features through-out. O'Kane's speech was audibly different from the other characters, a Munster man to their Connacht. The lyrical rhythms of the lines were underemphasized, the rounded cadences broken up by an improvisational, exploratory delivery: 'And I thinking you should have been living the like of a king of … Norway or … the Eastern World'. This naturalizing style worked well in the extremely violent final scenes, which avoided that awkwardness I found in the Druid production with its stop-go speech and action. But against the naturalizing of the speech and performances, the set represented a reversion to conventional picturesque. The small Cottesloe space was filled with a cutaway peasant cottage, well described by John Peter in his *Sunday Times* review:

> Robert Jones has designed a dingy interior, lit by fire and the odd candle, then by sunlight struggling through grimy window-panes. It could have been painted by some Dutch master like Brouwer or Ostade. Mark Henderson's lighting is important: observe how the light glints off the bottles and glasses on the shelf.[10]

Visually this was indeed genre scene, a study in the chiaroscuro effects of the homely, old-fashioned Irish cottage, all wood dressers and stone flagged floors. And that in turn corresponded to the condescending attitude of the reception. The *Daily Telegraph* reviewer complained that the set 'evokes a strong feeling of déjà vu' and that 'many of Synge's characters now seem like stock Oirish types rather than fresh-minted creations'.[11] There was a similar reaction from Alastair Macaulay in the *Financial Times*; in a review headed ' "Playboy" has the charm of the Oirish theatre', he remarked that 'The play's intense Irishness teeters on the brink of Oirishness'.[12]

The distinction is quite an interesting one in relation to both the London *Playboys* I have been discussing. There is an awareness on the part of the critics of the dangers of stage Irishry in

---

[10] John Peter, 'Playboy of the Western World', Sunday Times, 25 February 2001.

[11] Charles Spencer, 'A well-trodden trail, but lashings of atmosphere', *Daily Telegraph*, 21 February 2001.

[12] Alistair Macaulay ' "Playboy" has the charm of the Oirish theatre', 22 February 2001.

productions of Synge, the fakery stigmatized as 'Oirishness'. Bryden's production was congratulated as avoiding such excesses; Buffini's – in fact much lower key production – was suspected of 'Oirish' charm. But the 'intense Irishness' of Synge in all its essentialism is praised as something unquestionably authentic; none of the reviewers seem to have any sense that this too might be a theatrical cliché. The Irishness of the 1975 National production, heart-warming comedy that it was felt to be, may have been a way of exorcising the terrors of the real-life violence generated by the contemporary Irish situation. Yes, this was a play in which the father-killer was hero-worshipped for his deed by the Irish villagers, but the supposed parricide turns out to be a likeable lad and the father isn't really dead. The Druid *Playboy* of the 1980s represented another version of the play altogether, shorn of charm, earthed in the realities of material poverty, with an explosive violence not rendered harmlessly comic. Buffini in the 2001 National production to some extent followed the precedent set by Hynes with a darker *Playboy*, a more realized playing style. But still it could be consumed by London reviewers and audiences as at best 'intensely Irish', or more slightingly having the 'charm of the Oirish Theatre'. Within Ireland, where revivals of the play are frequent, some better than others, some innovative, some highly conventional, the arguments and critical evaluations are necessarily different. Whatever we may all feel about the latest Druid production directed by Garry Hynes, we do not commend it or condemn it for its Irishness.

6 | Roundtable Discussion with Garry Hynes

Lelia Doolan: I'd like to start the ball rolling by posing a question to Garry, about the politics of the first production, in 1907, which would have tremendous tumult of passion, on the part of those who were looking for a changed circumstance for Ireland, at a time when we had the shame of origin, hated the shape of ourselves, as portrayed in the West of Ireland, whether through a class or Unionist or republican point of view, where nowadays it is played not just as a piece of lyrical drama, but it is played as a strong, contradictory, and demanding view of ourselves. In the era of reality television, and a politics of confusion, where does the play belong, as opposed to 1982, in 2004, twenty-two years later?

Garry Hynes: I think in some sense that is up to the audience. It will do that. For me, I think sometimes that the fact that the play was so much part of something else, of its first era, has not been fair to the play itself. It is terribly difficult to get beyond *The Playboy of the Western World* as a play that everybody rioted at the Abbey over. As speakers today said, the play is complicated, contradictory, difficult … and great. You put yourself up against something that is absolutely huge. Sometimes the greatness of the play resides in the complicated, contrary challenge.

Ultan Macken: Why was it that you decided to celebrate Synge at this particular time?

Garry Hynes: Part of that is part of the answer to the last question. To me, Synge is an extraordinarily canonical writer, all of his work resonates through the theatrical tradition. Even his imperfect work, his unfinished work like *Deirdre of the Sorrows*. Sometimes he is defined more by his absence from our stage. In the theatre today, we need to have more of a sense of event, more of a sense of celebration. When you put it into that context, it makes sense to produce all of his creative work, particularly given that his canon is not very long; you could hardly do it with O'Casey. We eventually decided to start with *The Playboy*, his major work; we will see what happens to that production of *The Playboy* as we go along doing the other plays. When it comes to revive this production after doing the other plays, it will be very interesting to see what happens.

Jennifer Johnston: People have been talking almost as if the play is a changing factor. The play is the one factor that stands still. The society changes around it. We are coming into a huge, pagan, violent society, and this is a huge, pagan, violent play. There is also the thing, is it a comical tragedy or a comical tragedy, and this will be very much on the director's mind.

Garry Hynes: Well, it isn't really. You don't dance from one foot to the other. You just put your head down and do the play.

Lelia Doolan: In the early days, this was a great pagan play for a Victorian society with certain moral values which were quite narrow. It struck me that the pace and the delivery moved at hand gallop. People were speaking these lines as if they were everyday speech, that the movement and sense of reality was one of everydayness, rather than of a heightened reality. The tradition has sometimes been rather reverential. This production was very respectful but also very mellow, very funny, and very filmic – the stage pictures: the taller Jimmy, the smaller Philly, and all that business with that wonderful table. Did that evolve through production? The set itself was this huge box, immense, furnished with some very posh furniture. Take us through these realities.

Garry Hynes: If you talk about this approach being 'respectful', and in a manner of 'everyday reality', then that was not intended. That may be a part of the process – the production is not quite a week old yet. Things like Jimmy and Philly…well, in the first instance, the actors were cast as actors. I sometimes despair in casting that actors don't look like normal people. The reality is that you do see people like that – somebody is twice the size of somebody else. I remember a story about Paddy Dooley, who actually played Michael James in the production of 1982. He had a friend who was six foot four or five, and had a friend who was a dwarf. Paddy was coming home late one night. He heard two noises, men chatting away to each other, but only one pair of footsteps. It turns out that the big man was carrying the little one in his arms. And that story has always stayed in my head.

In terms of the furniture in the context of the design: one thing that always bothers me, once you design a set for the *The Playboy*, everybody in the auditorium knows what play is about to go on. I wanted to get away from that. The Ireland of that time seems now only to exist in stage terms, in the sense of the báinin, and the rough clothes, the fire and the bar, and the drinking and all that. It doesn't seem to have a connection to anything any longer, other than a connection to itself. If you go in for any kind of realism, which is what I want to go to, you have to go in for this *stage* realism. Synge was a Victorian. The play belongs to the mainstream, the European historical mainstream. Synge is also a European. Somehow I wanted to freshen the approach.

We have a back story for that as well. Pegeen's mother has always intrigued me. She is so not mentioned in the play, as Pegeen is essentially an orphan. Our story was that this furniture was her dowry in the marriage.

Lelia Doolan: Let's now do a quick 'whip-around' among the people who gave talks today. Well, Paige, do you want to start?

Paige Reynolds: I haven't seen as many productions of the play as people here. In fact, this is only the second production I've seen; the first was at Steppenwolf Theatre, and I thought it was remarkable. It was a lighter, more traditional version of the play than this one, and it wasn't at all invested in the European version of 'stage realism' that Garry alluded to. It was also less graphically violent, so it didn't have that threatening aspect of the 'stage Irish'. But it was certainly nostalgic, and even quaint – not qualities I saw in this Druid production, but ones that might have appealed to American audiences in Chicago.

I was intrigued by what Garry said about the back story for this production, about Pegeen being motherless. I've always been interested in why there are no mothers in this play; the closest we get is the scary wet nurse that Christy flees. The bleaker perspective of this *Playboy* called to mind, for me, other work like *Castle Rackrent* where the lack of mothers might be read as a signal that something's wrong with the society. The play resonated with other *Playboy*s, of course, but also with other work in the Irish canon.

I also found that the casting of Cillian Murphy, a young actor coming into his own, adds an interesting perspective to Christy's development in the play. You can see both the actor and the character move together from a naive sense of 'O my gosh, I've got a great part to play and a real audience!' to a sense of command and confidence. It makes you wonder if Murphy, with his Hollywood offers, will depart, like Christy, for the 'western world'.

Adrian Frazier: It seems to me that through Garry's recent work, before this production, audiences have seen Synge's importance to Irish theatre emerge. Synge is all through *The Leenane Trilogy*. Martin McDonagh may say he doesn't steal from Synge, but everyone else sees that he has done so in the Druid productions of his work. In Garry Hynes's rethinking of John B. Keane's plays, both Shakespeare and Synge come to the surface. In this show, Synge is seen both through Martin McDonagh and the reimagined John B. Keane. We are carried one step beyond Martin McDonagh, one step beyond John B. Keane, making Synge belong to the future. That has something to do with what Jennifer Johnston was saying, that we are now in a newly pagan world beyond old conceptions of Irishness. Once

The Playboy may have been rejected as stage-Irish, difficult to do satisfactorily, and rather an oddball in the canon. There is now, I should imagine, a capacity on the part of the audience, secure and wealthy, to reject at least the social and character stereotypes in the play as no longer having anything to do with them – sure, that world has nothing to do with us, weren't they all fools anyway? – so that *The Playboy* can be appreciated aesthetically, as a play, and not fatally entangled in identity issues.

Lelia Doolan: It will be interesting to see what happens when you take the play to Geesala, the townland that inspired the play's location. What will they think of the characters?

I wonder who it is that goes to theatre nowadays. I suppose Galway audiences are fairly middle-class; they'd have to be to pay for the tickets. People will come from the schools, because the play is on the curriculum. But does that part of the society that goes to the cinema go to the theatre?

Ultan Macken: It was very clever to cast Anne-Marie Duff and Cillian Murphy, because they are known to the young ones through the films.

Lelia Doolan: Ophelia Byrne, what were your impressions?

Ophelia Byrne: First, I should declare an interest: my partner Frankie McCafferty was in *Sharon's Grave*, and I still have a lot of that play in my head. That production made me consider John B. Keane anew, while this production of *The Playboy* made me look at theatre history itself again. There were echoes of *The Playboy* in *Sharon's Grave* that I had not previously perceived. You have the figure of the girl who is alone, deemed orphaned; the stranger who comes in from outside; you have the presence of the whole community and what they do and don't do, what is unacceptable in 1900 and what in the mid-twentieth century.

This made me think deeply about the canon, and about that particular controversy at the turn of the century. What I have heard again and again about the landmark Druid production of the 1980s – the realism of it, I think Nicky Grene called it 'dirty realism' – is that *The Playboy* showed us as we actually are and we were quite proud of that. This production revisits that production. When the curtain went up and the actors came on, it looked to me straightaway like one of the caricatures of Irish people in the turn-of-the-century *London Illustrated News*. It goes back to Victoriana and it goes back to the controversy the play once aroused. It says that what people objected to then is in fact still in the play. It is quite a brave thing to go back to those caricatures after having given the play dignity and status with the 1980s production. To me, this show repoliticizes the play. It reminds us of what people objected to in the first place. It asks: now how do you relate to it?

Lelia Doolan: Nicholas Grene, relating to what you were talking about earlier, the two London productions before and after the 1982 Druid production. The British response to Synge has been I think appalling. I was in the Siobhán McKenna production about which Adrian was speaking this morning. It had a good long run, but got headlines like 'Synge-Song'...rather patronizing. How do you think this version would fit into those London productions of which you spoke earlier?

Nicholas Grene: I don't know; I was intrigued to hear Garry say that the Victorian dimension was in her mind. Like other speakers, that's what I saw immediately on stage. We are back to things visually that are almost exactly what the Irish National Theatre movement was set up to combat – Samuel Lover, *Punch*, *Illustrated London News*, the big pictorial caricatured versions of Ireland. To put on stage those theatrical energies may be a way of challenging the somewhat condescending view of 'Oirishness'; at least, it is 'Oirishness' with a vengeance. This morning I was placing the 1982 Druid show as one that shifted the balance between one London production and another, shifting things toward a 'realizing' style. And had an effect on the 2001 National production and a more realistic style.

Of this show, we wondered, What will she do now? It comes as a sort of somersault, not to the realism of 1982, but to a style before 1907.

Jennifer Johnston: One thing I noted was the production cast aside the pantomime take on *The Playboy*, everybody in red petticoats and dancing the good dance on the stage. The time for that is well past. *Dancing at Lughnasa* is rather like that in the theatre: like going to a pantomime. I believe that it is probably a better play than it appeared –

Lelia Doolan: What is?

Jennifer Johnston: *Dancing at Lughnasa*. We know that *The Playboy* is a great play. It is great that Garry has not gone back to the realistic version of the 1980s, and also that she hasn't gone back to that pantomime, lyrical version.

Lelia Doolan: John Harrington, how do you think this production will travel?

John Harrington: I'd like to ask how it travels in time. The production was wonderful in the ways it addresses tradition. It works in increments. I too was caught up in how Philly and Jimmy were portrayed. In America throughout the twentieth century Jimmy and Philly are often played by semi-retired Abbey actors doing their usual turns. Here, in those two characters, the darker vision was very apparent. But when they came in after the wake, most of the audience around me seemed to be reacting to the way old Jimmy and Philly had been played, the physical comedy thing; whereas I wasn't seeing people acting out being drunk, but acting out alcoholism, or alcoholic poisoning – something much grimmer. This is a matter of increment. Jonathan Miller speaks of every production as a subsequent production, every one that is except a brand-new play, and a director addresses the traditions each time.

Garry, were you ever tempted by a radical approach, like setting it in Dublin flats? Now that would be making the play travel in time.

Garry Hynes: To be absolutely honest, that's not for me to do, John. No, one thing that hasn't changed in my perception of the play is that you have to have the physical walls of the house.

Outside is better left to the power of the imagination. So I started from four walls.

Bill McCormack: This production will remain in my mind for many reasons, acting, directing, and interpretation. But one thing that was very obvious was the visual image of the set. I don't think I could describe it as realism, rather an extraordinary kind of psychological representation of a state of mind and social state, with an almost metallic exterior, like verdigris which has been dripping down the walls, a long industrial like pillar which goes down the center of the set. This is of course very different, obviously, from the cottage, the thatch, the window on the sea. What it does for me is that it brings the play into Europe. This is a play that is in touch with things like *Nosferatu*. Jimmy Cullen could get a part in a remake of *Nosferatu*. It also seems to link up with notions of degeneration and domestic and social violence, not necessarily of the fisticuffs kind, but other kinds of social violence. What is constant is this verdigris image. Everything else is shifting and changing, the pace, even the characterization. But there is this constant single image, which is anxious and anxious-making. Whoever is responsible collectively or individually for this image deserves to be congratulated.

Garry Hynes: Well, it is everybody really: myself, and Francis O'Connor…Davy Cunningham, who had to light the show from the front, because it is a roof set with only two small apertures in it.

Lelia Doolan: I think the opening of the second act was particularly stunning, with the light through the window, and the light through the door, a spring day *par excellence*, and the whole of that growth is being brought up by the sun, the growth of Christy and the growth of the play.

Mary King: I would like to follow on from what Bill McCormack was saying. I think that young people ought to see the play. Christy is a youth who is abused – he is abused, in flight, frightened, closed in, claustrophobic. It is a play which is beginning to address us as we need to see ourselves, an Ireland which was suppressed, and which people continue to attempt to suppress.

Garry Hynes: In terms of trying to work out what happened with the riots, this time I was really struck by how offensive the play could be taken to be. I was saying to Kathy Strachan, however hard we try, we are not going to go as far as he did, because he's gone so far. I have always believed it is not the *shifts* line, but an accumulation of tension in that audience that couldn't cope.

Lelia Doolan: How brutal and graphic certain lines are! – 'and he blackened from his beatings like a tinker's ass'.

Ophelia Byrne:: I did find myself at certain times looking at those characters – Jimmy and Philly – and their buffoonery, the excess of it, and saying to myself, well, now hang on a minute. And if I felt that way in the twenty-first century, that is a mild inkling of how people must have felt in 1907, and of how angry they got. This production succeeds in re-injecting a sense of the original offensiveness of the play to a degree. But I wonder if the audience around me got that sense of offence, because those around me in the theatre seemed to feel only enjoyment.

Paige Reynolds: But there was so much in the play that audience members could choose to identify with whatever they wanted. At one moment, I believe when Christy was first pummelled by the villagers, I was thinking 'This is so dark!' – but the woman in front of me was laughing uproariously.

Lelia Doolan: This is a playwright who is a comical craftsman, and knows what he is doing in every moment. Look at how each of the first two acts ends with a laugh line; in Act One Christy's 'Wasn't I the foolish fellow not to murder my father in the days gone by?' and Widow Quin at the end of Act Two: 'Well, if the worst comes in the end of all, it'll be great game to see there's none to pity him but a widow woman, the like of me, has buried her children and destroyed her man.'

Adrian Frazier: I got the impression that a lot of the production arose from the actors, as if the director had said, All right, you two fellows, you get to play vicious imbeciles, and you also get to be drunk for half of the show. God, they said, I'd love to play drunk for half the play! Then the director may have said, You fellows get to work with the rope, and be pulling on that rope for quite some time. O, actors replied, I could really have fun with that rope. The table is there, the director says, and we can use the levels of the table and higher level of the high window.

How many times did one actor or another get up on that table? The actors were released into devising good gags on stage, and they saw in the play where such gags had been planted by the playwright. Many earlier productions have been acted under literary restraint. In such productions, the cast were saying the lines and doing the parts, but they detheatricalized the play by accentuating its literariness. Here the actors did a very good job of thwarting the metrical impulse of the lines, of stopping them, or slowing them down, by inventing different kinds of business within speeches, so that the lyrical impulse wouldn't gather its own velocity, to the detriment of the pro-duction's theatricality.

Garry Hynes: There was a deliberate drive to do that – especially to constitute the table as a second stage. It is such a broad play about play, from changes of costume over and again, to the speeches to one another. Coming out of this rehearsal process, I was very conscious of it as a piece of craft, a piece of art. Before, I was conscious of the sheer drive and energy; this time of the extraordinary craft.

Irina Ruppo: I thought it was interesting that the casting of the Widow Quin not as an old woman as in the McKenna film, but as young woman, emphasized her importance, almost more than that of Pegeen, and shifted the audience's sympathy to the Widow, and brought out the tragic nature of this production.

Garry Hynes: The thing is though, when we did it twenty years ago, with Marie Mullen, about that age at the time, there was a huge amount of attention to the fact of her relative youth. But the fact is, the age is given in the script, as a woman about thirty.

It is the theatrical tradition that a mature actress would move to character parts, and the Widow was such a character part.

Niall Buggy as Christy, Siobhán McKenna as the Widow Quin, from a 1976 production

Photograph from Christopher Fitz-Simon, The Irish Theatre

Lelia Doolan: It is also true that a star actress, like Siobhán McKenna, in the Pegeen role, skewed the production, so that it became the Playgirl of the Western World. This production settles into the right relationships, it is *The Playboy* of the Western World.

I wanted to ask you about the staging of the last scene, which I regard as the Mt Everest, the Kilimanjaro, and the Cliffs of Moher all in one: it has comedy, farce, tragedy, romance, but in that rope scene, there are just too many lines!

Garry Hynes: No, there are not. You may get that feeling watching this production, but that is because it hasn't settled yet.

I actually think the first act is more difficult. There you put down the foundation for the entire production. That is really difficult, where you go from his fear to his delight at being potboy. You have to get the audience there to buy into the production.

'The Rope Scene' in Act Three. Cillian Murphy holding on to the table; Gary Raymond as Shawn Keogh at the head of the rope

Photograph: Keith Pattison

Lelia Doolan: But still the rope scene is difficult; why is that?

Garry Hynes: The trick of the rope is itself difficult. The text says Christy wraps his legs around the table. But the fact is that no matter how drunk they are those men could pull him at least as far as the door. Therefore locking his legs around the table isn't an option so far as credibility goes. That's why we had the chain around the table. You don't want to lose credibility with the audience at the moment that Pegeen comes up with the sod of turf to burn his legs off the table, or else she is doing that gratuitously. If it is clear that she doesn't need to do that, then it changes her character. And she at the same time has to go through her turnaround.

Ophelia Byrne: The Widow Quin is reinvented as a woman who has power on the stage. Quite a lot of the time, the stage is hers: she is alone on it. She may be on the margins, sitting on the side, but she has cut deals, and she knows what she wants, and if she doesn't get it she is not going to be left high and dry. I haven't seen that in other productions, it is an extremely interesting approach and O'Sullivan's portrayal was really quite extraordinary.

It would be a shame, however, if we wrapped up without a word about Cillian Murphy too, because he turns in such a complex, fine and physical performance. It is quite something

Cillian Murphy as Christy about to go out the door at the play's end.

Photograph: Keith Pattison.

to see such classic Irish drama done in such a physical way. Garry Hynes' work with choreographer David Bolger is seriously paying dividends, because this production really moves. What looks initially like a straightforward box-set becomes a multi-layered creation with movement taking place all over it, a table being used to give a second level, and a window to provide a third; even the table itself is kept moving. And an actor like Cillian, who relishes the physical challenges, can obviously swing with that. The change from the first scene, where he's so small and frightened, to the last where he is just huge and expansive in gesture, is magnificent – he's not just saying it, he *is* it.

Lelia Doolan: Well, Garry, has the response of people today reinforced what you were doing? Has it been useful to you?

Garry Hynes: It has been fascinating and will be useful. This production is going into repertory, and things have arisen in the rehearsal process, and in responses this past week and today, that will be useful when we come back to *The Playboy* in a year's time.

Lelia Doolan: I want to thank Garry and NUI Galway MA in Drama and Theatre for this conference today. Sometimes events are allowed to pass without the praise they deserve and the recognition that this audience has given to your production of *The Playboy*.

PLAYBOY 2004: EIGHT VIEWS

1 | Terrible Truths, of our own making

Ophelia Byrne

> In a way there are two plays, one within another, and unless the inner one is seen, I am not surprised at the screaming about the outer one, which in itself is repellent, and must so remain until seen in the light of the conception out of which it arises …

This perceptive comment from 'Pat' in *The Irish Times* about the original production captures the conundrum that is *The Playboy of the Western World.* The play holds within it two impulses: one, the very raw human condition of a small rural community facing some all-too-real hardships, and the other the drive towards exuberant, uncompromising, highly theatrical and bawdy comedy and language which engendered such suspicion on the play's first outings. Despite 'Pat's' appeals, the one was initially not seen in the light of the other; audiences could not get past that 'repellent' outer shell to view what he contemporaneously perceived as the true core. Perhaps not until Garry Hynes's landmark 1980's Druid production was the play finally so viewed when, successfully turning the work inside out, Hynes succeeded in creating space for the inner play to be seen first. The result was a production so striking that some have chosen to retain this as their definitive *Playboy*, opting not to sully their impression of the work with subsequent versions. And so the decision of the director herself to revisit the play in 2004 presents its own interesting conundrum. Post her own landmark production, and post the often unremarkable offerings of the work in Ireland since, what is left today for audience or director to discover in the canonical *Playboy of the Western World*?

That Hynes's answer seems to be that of twenty-first century shock seems peculiarly appropriate. For if the premiere Playboy production was praised for its capacity to reveal 'truly terrible truths, of our own making, which we dare not face for the present', the play has in key productions since displayed a similar capacity. The original 1907 'terrible truth' lay not in the word 'shifts', but in the fact that Home Rule or no, a self-promoted Irish Ireland notion of 'Celtic impeccability' was self-evidently being belied by social realities; drunkenness, poverty, loneliness and repressed sexuality all existed, even if the admission of such was difficult. 'It is as if we looked in a mirror for the first time and found ourselves hideous', mused 'Pat', 'We fear to face the thing.'

By the early 1980s, however, and through that most tumultuous decade of social argument, such hideousness was staring us in the face. We feared everything. Dole queue figures, like the statistics of emigration, unmarried mothers, abortions, Troubles' casualties, whirled like so much demented shifting social confetti before the eyes of those still left to see them. Add a soundtrack mixing the eerie endless whispers of desperate Gay Byrne radio listeners with Geldof's brutally splenetic 'Banana Republic', and whether attacking or defending Irish Ireland in its last convulsive days of domination, the now-aging *Playboy* seemed hardly likely to feature. The terrible truths were all too evident.

And yet *The Playboy* did feature, to such a degree that it is talked of since. When Hynes' 1980s Playboy mirror was held up to audiences, what they remember was not hideousness, but beauty; the 'terrible truth' was that despite the enduring socio-political traumas of Ireland, theirs was also an inheritance of tough, darkly humorous, enduring humanity, now all but forgotten. If initially shocked at the reminder, audiences soon came in droves to stare bewildered and relieved at themselves. 'And to think it's me talking sweetly', wondered Pegeen, and we wondered with her at an intimate production which notably, in a period characterized by shame, anger and disappointment, reduced a 'parade of grotesques to a manageable roomful of quare fellows with whom we become, for the duration of the piece, convivial' (*The Times*). The highly realistic piece offered an experience in which one could 'smell the straw, sweat and beer' from the closely observed period set, and hear lyrical language which was almost scored to ring out from performers 'like a song' (*New York Times*). Humour might be noted, and indeed skilfully achieved, but this was not alone the substance of the piece; the 'inner' play came first, created through painstaking, delicately naturalistic detail, and the production was celebrated as such. Yes, we were and we were happy to be.

Thus *The Playboy* kick-started a pilgrimage of rediscovery for audiences with Druid, particularly in its Galway home and in the work of Tom Murphy. As audiences found themselves either physically and/or mentally confronted by the painful journey from rural to urban, Druid offered a series of acutely perceptive productions treading the tightrope between the two. This culminated in the masterpiece *Bailegangaire*, a vital coming-to-terms with the by-now fiercely contested Irish notions of home, tradition and family, but also encompassed the terror of Famine, the savagery of *A Whistle in the Dark* and the loneliness of *Conversations on a Homecoming*. In their company, *Playboy* sat in the Druid repertoire with ease as a founding father and modern contemporary. Itself dignifiedly and thoughtfully embodying the pain of straddling old and new worlds simultaneously, the play's various Druid incarnations brought a newly urbanized, transitional, edgy generation to the Irish theatre in the 1980s, and Murphy's contemporary work then kept them there.

By the 1990s, however, what Druid's *Playboy* had pioneered and brokered in the 1980s was now more confidently sought for mass cultural audiences. There was first, the Janus-like Robinson Presidency, both outwardly European and self-assuredly Irish; then, too, came the meeting of tradition and modernity in Riverdance, and the disbelief and subsequent familiarity of its international success as such. The developing Celtic Tiger economy's name indicated a mix of the contemporary and historic; so too did the rollercoaster Northern Ireland peace process, with the Good Friday Agreement accommodating past and present to look towards the future. In these circumstances, it seemed wrong to attribute the term 'extravaganza' simply to a play by Synge; with the mélange of ancient and modish at its core, the entire country seemed to have become an extravaganza of success. Martin McDonagh's ironic and hugely successful *Leenane Trilogy* perhaps best encapsulated the spirit of the moment; described as J.M. Synge meets Quentin Tarantino, its 'almost postmodern recollection of Irish drama in the last century' (Michael Billington), and not pure Synge, seemed right for the age. As audiences revelled in McDonagh's work, drunk and dazed on the new Ireland of excess, their laughter was that of both recognition and relief. Apparently no longer embattled as a society, McDonagh's plays spoke of times which could now comfortably be acknowledged as bygone, but had the refreshing spark of a knowing post-modern contextualization.

Today, in the very early years of the new century, this again no longer seems enough. Apparent fault lines beneath that easy blend of past and present are becoming exposed: the peace process stuttering, Riverdance scaled down, the Celtic Tiger's roar no longer dominant. The rollercoaster experience is moving from exhilaration to exhaustion: far from being easy, the struggling Irish physical infrastructure alone describes the actual tough realities of the old/new transition being attempted, while the post-modern seems to offer cold comfort. The present situation seems difficult to call, and before its challenge, Hynes has once again offered something unexpected: not new writing, curiously, but a revisiting of Irish classics for a twenty-first century, starting with her acclaimed re-workings of John B. Keane's *Sive* and *Sharon's Grave*, and now moving to Synge.

The Keane seems highly appropriate. For too long ignored by professional theatre, Keane's work now appears to accommodate and almost delight in Hynes' idiosyncratic approach, mining its darker seams whilst allying his distinctive language with highly physical, European traditions of theatre. Offering extraordinarily bleak cautionary tales of what can happen in worlds dominated by monetary concerns, and where the soul and imagination is ignored, the immediacy of the works for a contemporary audience is both subtle yet evident. Working off great blank canvases of sets, as in *Sharon's Grave*, the traditional items which remain are like reminders of or passports to a world where greasy tills, land and houses are of pre-eminent importance; where God is departed or absent; where even decent travellers or 'foreigners' are unwelcome and suspect; where the less-than-perfect of mind or body are similarly suspect; where families despite their own best efforts are being broken apart; but where redemption while unlikely is not impossible.

The resonances here are plain and need little adornment: the shock or 'terrible truth' is the contemporary undercurrent in pieces now some four decades old. This serves as a reminder that Ireland has been here before and any contemporary thematic echoes are, and should be, deeply uncomfortable. Hynes however leaves little opportunity to avoid such discomfort: *Sharon's Grave*, for example, was uncompromisingly stripped back rather than gilded, and its modernity underscored by every aspect of the production, from design to movement and performance style.

To come to *Playboy* in this manner is rather more daring, however. Better known than its Keane counterparts, for many the central play of the Irish canon, there is also the issue of that landmark production: how to better it? How even to match it? Hynes's answer in essence is to abandon it, and follow her own current reworking impulses, rather than her past creation. And the result is startling. Here, what greets one is again, a great blank canvas set in the shape of an enormous high box, and again, there are the token objects: a huge table, a large clock, a dominant storm light, a hard plain settle-bed, and an open fire-place like a half-remembered thing, sitting centre-stage surrounded by blank space. But unlike *Sharon's Grave*, the effect is not Spartan: instead, as the curtain goes up, what is revealed is the living embodiment of an Irish shebeen straight from the pages of the nineteenth century *London Illustrated News*. Just as in that publication's steel engravings, smoke billows in a shadowy cavernous blurry space; a candle glimmers through the gloom; and as the eyes accustom themselves to the darkness, strange and contextually bewildering objects reveal themselves. Here is a grand chair with a footstool, surely too grand for our modern impression of a shebeen? And there a fine chiming clock which Pegeen winds: again, do we believe in its contextual veracity?

Almost before a word is spoken, then, our understanding of *The Playboy*'s world has been thoroughly queried, and lest we miss the reference, Victorian-style piano music plinks emphatically in the background. This, we infer, is a *Playboy* to be viewed not immediately through our own eyes, but first through a prism of its own times; when characters enter extraordinarily garbed in top hats and frock coats, that suspicion intensifies. The subsequent arrival of Philly and Jimmy as a highly physical, visually extraordinary, extended music-hall double-act of Irish buffoonery, hints at a deeper ambition however, and on their return from the wake this is confirmed. Too inebriated to properly stand or even speak, they embark on a lengthy exaggerated comedy routine of excessive drunkenness, literally crawling along walls and hanging off doors; as they do, it finally becomes clear that this no mere period setting, but a deliberate, sharp and acutely informed take on that period. What Hynes appears to be attempting is an inversion of her 1980s efforts, turning the play inside out once again; the result is a production which focuses on the other, the outer *Playboy*, and to ask how we as audiences interpret it as such today.

For in this production, the play is arguably as much *Potboy* as *Playboy*, as much the play 'Pat' found 'repellant' as that 1980s audiences found lovely. It features characters as hard as those the 1907 *Irish News* perceived; the Widow Quin is no ageing sad-eyed crone, but an astute operator with an eye to self-preservation; Mahon not a twinkling charmer, but a tough-talking swaggerer; Pegeen Mike far from an enchanting firebrand, and instead a small fierce bundle of ordinary frustrations. This *Playboy*'s comedy is of the 'low and vulgar type' as noted by the 1907 *Irish Times*; the village girls are awkward, exaggerated, squealing creatures; Shawn Keogh haplessly creeps along floors; Philly and Jimmy undertake several routines of comic gormlessness; the Widow Quin stomps about, hands stuffed in pockets, with a deliberately exaggerated gait. The dialogue indeed seems 'coarse ... as if the author had set himself to find out exactly how much his audience would stand'; Aisling O'Sullivan as the Widow issues barbarous screeches in various comic voices, while general accents vary and speech rhythms stretch and contract in unexpected places. And so little by little, as the picture accumulates, what emerges is less the roomful of quare fellows so comforting in the 1980s, and more the parade of grotesques described by the original protesters. The convivial room-fellows of old acquaintance are transformed to an astonishing farrago of outlandish souls; it is an extraordinary undertaking.

For on first viewing, the production is a puzzle-the-world. It is not that the tendencies played to extremity in this production are not latent in the play itself. If anything, the production proves that much the original viewers complained of is indeed inherent in *Playboy*, and that to play the work in this way is actually to unsmother some of its elements. Philly and Jimmy's post-wake dialogue is revealed anew by the carefully choreographed comedic staging; Christopher Mahon's own transformation is stunningly revealed when allied to a thrilling physical playing of the role; a welcome blow-torch is taken by the style of production to the traditional role of the Widow Quin, burnishing her role and status to something quite strange and powerful. More complex, however, is the relationship between this radical staging and the play's central characters. For audiences accustomed to viewing *The Playboy* as predominantly a lyrical love-story, the production is highly challenging: the focus is skewed away from Pegeen and Christy, and shared amongst the community itself. And for those whose chief attraction is that song-like scored language, so beloved in the 1980s production, there will likewise be discomfort: from the sometimes deliberately strangled voices of Philly and Jimmy, to the Widow Quin's swooping bellow, the lyrical, much like the entire play, is almost jolted out of familiarity.

Little wonder, then, that this production has hit a nerve. If there were many who laughed uproariously throughout, there were also those who had a sharp, almost visceral recoil from the production; this was not, some disapprovingly noted after the production, a 'proper' *Playboy* at all. In the sense they imply, they were right. This is a *Playboy* of chutzpah, not concession; not easy on the contemporary world, but seeking to square up to it and grab it by the lapels. As such, it is respectful to playwright rather than punter, and seems designed to provoke; that it grins in the process even as it does so takes none of the venom from what it has to say. Because this is a savagely critical production. Its directorial style liberates the play from the restyled Celtic impeccability of recent years to show a people both hard and cruel, whose easy warmth masks a brutal business sense, and whose love of fun co-exists with a steely sense of self-preservation. The community's adoration of fame, glamour and spin is only matched by its own capacity for self-deception; as such, lacking any sense of self-awareness, it finds itself very lovely indeed, and has no conception that the overall combination might be repulsive. We gaze, mesmerized, at the outcome, but the more the production continues the more relentless the picture becomes. With a growing sense of unease, we begin to dissociate from the depiction, and the stronger the portrayal, the more the instinct to uncouple ourselves from it. But try as we might, the 'mighty gap' is simply not there: though we stare into the mirror and hope not to see ourselves, an increasingly clear reflection grimaces happily back. And worst of all, it does so with such infectious, hideous delight that it demands we join in despite ourselves; we are asked not only that we find ourselves, but that we enjoy this picture too.

The result overall is deeply discomforting. No new play of the Celtic Tiger has succeeded in truly eviscerating the bling-bling nature of the society created during his reign, and this production goes no small way towards achieving precisely that. Its extreme style demands response; its grotesquery invites rejection; its mirror asks us to find out who and what we have become and in reversing from this portrayal, to locate ourselves in the process. And to a degree it succeeds. The irony of sitting in an audience watching the lurid desperation of Christy's on-stage audience to transcend mundanity by finding someone to carry their dreams, is unnerving; the luminous presence of Cillian Murphy alone asks discomfiting questions of us and underscores unappealing parallels. The emphasis on the community as such in this production therefore seems entirely right: our 'terrible truth' is that despite our advances, we often sit cruelly well within the extravagances of this 'parade of grotesques'. To that extent, this production repeats the effort of its progenitor: it shows us to ourselves as hideous, and asks if we fear to face that truth.

The answer to this seems varied. In 1907, as in 2004, there were those who rejected the playing out of hand. In 1907, as in 2004, there were those who found the production provocative in a 'slow burn' way, sparking thought and reflection long after the play. But unlike 1907, there may be one major difference. In 2004, were there those who simply rolled along with the laughter, who despite the radicalness of the presentation simply dissociated themslves from its comment and took only the humour? The suspicion is that there were; and while this is a probable response, it is also a curious one. Its evocation arises not from any soft indulgence in production; this *Playboy* could scarcely go any further down its chosen path, and is quite sharply extreme as it is. The issue instead seems one of audience itself. It may be that the Celtic Tiger has indeed transformed us into that people described in the glossy brochures of official Ireland: easy, relaxed, our sense of self-identity now so solid on its modern European ground that it cannot be challenged. Or it may, conversely, be that we have become so sluggishly inured by prosperity that we simply cannot think or view ourselves critically, even before the most fierce of efforts.

If the former is preferred, the latter seems more accurate. Patently, though we are more at home with ourselves, we are not yet at one with our own glossy picture; patently, though we have made progress, it has not been without cost and is not yet completed. If in the 1980s, we needed Druid's *Playboy* to be able just to look ourselves in the eye, it may be that in 2004, we are beyond truly seeing ourselves at all, having fallen completely in love with our own reflection. Hence, the 'terrible truth' this production throws up may not simply be that of our grotesquery, difficult enough as that is. It may also be that of our unpreparedness, despite due warning, for what would happen should the Celtic Tiger, that entrancing stranger of gallous stories and dirty deeds, indeed depart. For what *Playboy* in 2004 ultimately says is that a community, having happily deluded itself, can nonetheless be abandoned; the ditching of all critical faculties for a brief, wonderful moment can have serious consequences. 'But don't they get to stay together? Surely that can't be the end?' gasped one young viewer aghast as the curtain came down at the Dublin performance. And we all smiled wryly, even as Pegeen's final cry of loss and unknowing echoed through the theatre, and the community stared in disbelief at the trail of on-stage wreckage. Because surely, that is not us on stage. Surely the belief that something is so, makes it so. And surely, the good times will last forever if we can all just keep on laughing.

2 | Postmodern Paddywhackery

Adrian Frazier

A Druid production in Galway, a city of 70,000, is a big event. This is a star-studded cast in a production directed by the home-town hero. Hundreds of thousands of euro have been spent on it. On opening night, search-lights revolved their beams in the sky outside the theatre. Photographers waited on the steps to shoot personalities – university presidents, actors, town councilors, and members of the old Druid company – arrive for the debut. The television cameraman and presenter Orla Nicks from RTE by their presence guaranteed to the audience the national importance of the event.

The spectator's first impression is of the vastness of the stage. The full depth, width, and height of the Town Hall playing area is used. There is no sense of a low-ceilinged, cramped shebeen. There's no bar, no mantled hearth. The standard *Playboy* set is not here.

The doors and walls are all alike mottled, streaky, uneven, and, in this light, as green as a sea-cave. Centre stage toward the back on a slight ledge is an open brazier with smoking sods of turf. An iron mast that holds the crane and pots over the fire goes right up to the planked roof, where an opening draws the smoke up and out.

On the right between the door and the brazier is an armchair and stool, Victorian, with curved wooden arms and legs and an upholstered seat. Behind that, and against the wall, is a rather elegant piece of furniture serving as a washstand. On the right hand wall, the door is at the back, and toward the apron of the stage is a church-pew or settle-bed with its back to the wall.

To the left of the fire, and the most prominent thing on the whole stage, is a long wooden table with stout carved legs. Pegeen (Anne-Marie Duff) sits at this table, facing center, and writing out her shopping list. Her hair in a tight bun, she is wearing a pale-yellow Victorian dress down to the floor, with a boned and fitted top, cream-coloured and embossed – elegant. She is not wearing the red skirts of all the Pegeens that came before her. In the social scheme of rural Ireland this Pegeen is a woman of fortune, accustomed to posting orders for consumer goods, and aware of fashions created far from cottage looms.

Shawn Keogh (Gary Lydon) arrives. Greasy hair parted, he wears a black vested suit with a swallow-tail coat. Stooped and cringing – as he will be throughout – he turns and turns in his nervous hands the brim of a top-hat. He looks like an engravature illustrating an 1890s *Punch* cartoon about Ireland.

Next to enter is Michael James O'Flaherty with his retinue, Philly and Jimmy. The relative size of things plays tricks here. The doorway is undersized, so the actor playing Michael James (Eamon Morrissey) fills it, and he is not a tall man. It is roomy for the short actor playing Philly (David Pearse), but impossibly low for the six-footer playing Jimmy (Chris O'Dowd). This initial framing by the doorway alters our perceptions of size on stage, and that illusion is sustained by other artifices. For instance, throughout the next scene, tall Jimmy and small Philly stand next to one another. Both of them are warming themselves beside the fire while supporting themselves by the crane, and Jimmy reaches right over Philly's head to take the highest hold. One looks like a leprechaun, the other like an oafish Irish giant – both comically cretinous.

They have a good hard laugh at Shawn Keogh for being afraid of spending the night alone in the public house with his fiancée Pegeen Mike. His future father-in-law joins in the nasty merriment in his customarily stagey fashion. So terrified is Shawn Keogh, that he crawls rapidly all across the loose turf floor from near the door to the apron of the stage, looking very like a squealing pig going on its trotters as fast as it can, trying to escape three farmers ready to butcher him. Then Shawn Keogh crawls back to the center, faces the audience, kneels, and prays, still clutching and twisting his hat. It is a disgusting image of piety. The 'audience' behind him laugh; some in the real audience in front of him laugh too. Pegeen, however, does not. She is angry with her father long before the mockery is complete, and Shawn has fled, leaving his coat in the hands of Michael James. It is a strange adumbration of the flagellation scene at the play's end.

The interrogation of Christy Mahon is interestingly done. Jimmy, Philly, and Shawn Keogh sit on the bench against the right wall, in profile from the audience's point of view. Christy Mahon is sitting beside the fire, hunched over a bit, getting warm. Michael James is in his upholstered chair between Christy and the others, while Pegeen is way over to the left, with an arm on the porter-barrel – so the actors are widely scattered on the stage. The inquiries begin after a bit of silence, and casually, like conversation in a quiet pub. The questions are cast across the long space of the stage. At first, they are not asked or answered with much urgency, but then interest picks up in the guessing-game, as if Christy is playing at riddles. Jimmy, excited, gets up to change places on the bench with Philly, in order to get closer. He even rises to his feet and steps forward in order to pose his question about whether the young fellow on the run had gone fighting for the freedom of the Boers. Finally, Pegeen loses patience and strides across the diagonal of the whole stage – as she jeers, 'You're only saying it' – and picks up the broom from the corner. She raises it high while she crosses back to stage centre as if to strike Christy a big sweeping blow. The particular gesture gives a sense to Christy's exclamation – 'I killed my father…for doing the like of that' – and prefigures the blow of the loy that will so often be reconfigured later in the play.

There is the inevitable and probably necessary long moment of silence after Christy's admission and the outcries and genuflections that follow it. People exchange questioning glances. It is Michael James's part as host to say something. Upon consideration, he concludes that it is possible that every murderer might have good reason for his deed. That opens the door a crack to the fantastical turn in fortune for Christy. It opens wider still when without blinking the villagers accept as sufficient explanation Christy's jabber that his father was getting old and crusty so Christy could not put up with him at all. There does not seem to be any way through this dizzying implausibility for the actors but wide-eyed obliviousness to the implausibility. That is what happens here. The crowd is soon off to fantasizing how the deed was done, with Michael James ham-acting with a lunge and a twist when he imagines that 'It was with a hilted knife maybe?'

Although this problem may be solved as the players settle into their roles, Aisling O'Sullivan is so good as the Widow Quin she makes the other performers – very good in themselves – look only so-so by comparison. Worse, she just about acts Anne-Marie Duff off the stage.

Aisling O'Sullivan as the Widow Quin; Cillian Murphy as Christy Mahon; Act Two.

Photograph: Keith Pattison.

Aisling O'Sullivan is a tall, beautiful woman of thirty; she is not the middle-aged, heavy-dugged, blowsy, over-the-hill comedienne of many earlier versions of the Widow. Though her long red hair has been ratted and jumbled, and she clomps about in boots below her long skirts, pulling an auburn shawl tightly round her shoulders, there is just so much life in her eyes, her countenance, and in the sashaying of her walk, one has to like her.

The way O'Sullivan plays the opening scene, the Widow fancies the stranger at first sight. She is lonely, and wants a man in her houseen. Even if Christy is a bit of a baby from her point of view (a woman who knows sex, has had children, and killed her husband), she will be able to enjoy life with him, her baby boy, her man, and her colleague in deeds of blood. When she strides over to a chair by the table, sprawls into it, pulls another chair close, and eyeing Christy, stamps her boot on the seat of the open chair as a signal for him to come, we see the whole relationship in a picture. She also does a very clever piece of acting when she's telling Christy to come sleep at her house, not in the shebeen where he works. She does not look at Christy, but, smiling brightly and competitively, at Pegeen. In this love triangle, the two fine women are not just waiting for Christy to pick one or the other; they are fighting each other for him, and the Widow Quin has the edge on Pegeen in sexual confidence. By Act Two, however, she comes to find she is going to lose the battle for Christy, and from there out O'Sullivan never fails to show, at the back of all her further scheming, that she's sad to have lost him. It is an amazingly deep and psychologically unified characterization.

The minor male roles – Jimmy, Philly, and Michael James – are not deep. They are played in an exaggerated postmodern comic style, as grotesques, and drunken grostesques at that. When Jimmy and Philly enter at the start of Act Three, the stage direction indicates that they are 'slightly drunk' after Kate Cassidy's wake. In this production, the two are frankly shit-faced. Chris O'Dowd, as Jimmy the giant, walks as if on stalks, with knees locked and arms straight out, reeling this way and that. David Pearse, as Philly the leprechaun, can only stay upright by keeping a firm grip on the door jamb with one hand, while his body swings through the door in an arc until he comes right around to the wall. He remains plastered there in fear of the infinite, unsupported spaces of the wider room. Michael James also enters fluthered, and Eamon Morrissey draws upon decades of professional experience in playing the Irish drunk on stage for the enactment.

In earlier productions of the play, actors often simply establish that they have 'a drop taken', and then play the subsequent action straight. In this version, the three boys never let one forget that they are hard put to it to cope with any difficulties at all, so thoroughly drunk are they. The overall effect of having the rest of the play proceed with three actors on stage doing simultaneous star-turns as Irish stage-drunks, if not stage-Irish drunks, is reminiscent of the chaos that descends upon the cast in a Martin McDonagh play. In spite of the big-gestured, nineteenth century melodramatic acting by the three, they also give off a contemporary air of male menace, especially when Philly and Jimmy follow Old Mahon out the door in hopes of not just hearing about bloodshed, but seeing some. Should anyone fall to the ground in a fight, they look like the type – common enough today – who would kick a man in the head, just for the hell of it.

In the middle of all this, Cillian Murphy and Anne-Marie Duff strive to play out a romantic love story. Photogenic and subtle on the big screen, Murphy is also a resourceful, high-energy actor on stage. His playing style here is bravura. He accomplishes a variety of picturesque moments along the self-fashioning pilgrimage of Christy: the sheepish little boy, the lad tickled to death that two fine women are fighting over him, the self-infatuated flirt with the flock of village girls, the cock-of-the-walk in Shawn Keogh's new swallow-tail suit and tophat, the winning jockey in a golden jersey, and the oppressed son on all fours sobbing in memory of how awful it is for a boy to have a strong father. What lies beneath that might connect all these points was unclear to me.

Anne-Marie Duff kept her hands clenched and all the muscles in her body flexed through most of the night, relaxing just once, when Christy and Pegeen have their love-scene centre stage, facing one another, on their knees and holding hands.

Anne-Marie Duff as Pegeen, Cillian Murphy as Christy, in love scene from Act Three

Photograph: Keith Pattison

That was lovely, but it did not suffice for me as a rendering of 'the one great love' of a life. The sexual contact between them was not missing, nor was it sufficiently present. The two do some excellent sinuous mirroring of one another's postures and expressions – the courtship rites of homo sapiens – but the tradition that all their words of passion result in just one kiss is kept up in this contemporary production. The one soft kiss Anne-Marie Duff as Pegeen gives Christy before her father returns from the wake is supposed to climax adequately a great deal of yearning, but does it? It may have served in 1907, and constituted the maximum tenderness allowed on a public stage, but in 2004 we want to see her go too far with Christy to turn back without terrible shame.

Once Michael James returns, and is persuaded to give the two lovers his blessing, they kneel holding hands at one side of the big table, and he like a priest solemnizes their union from the other side. Just then, bloody-headed Old Mahon (Frank O'Sullivan) charges in, drags Christy down on the dirt floor, and thwacks him loudly with his blackthorn. The next lines are run very quickly, with Mahon, Christy, and the Crowd all getting in their bits pell-mell. Only seconds pass before Pegeen is saying, in full voice, baying with the other hounds, 'Take him on from this, for I think bad the world should see me raging for a Munster liar and the fool of men.' If one happened to be fixing one's eyes upon Anne-Marie Duff through this scene, it was impossible to trace in her lineaments just how she went so rapidly from pledging her troth to sending her man away. It is a difficult and compressed transition – perhaps as hard for an actress as virtuoso passages in a Pagannini concerto are for a violinist. No doubt, there are dozens of ways to do it, or attempt it, but this way revealed a problem in the playtext, rather than solving that problem.

Stylistically, the two most attractive things about the ensemble's playing are the flamboyant physicality of the movement and the deliberately un-rhythmical way of saying Synge's lines.

The players exploit the theatrical potential of everything on the stage. The table becomes a second stage: Philly and Jimmy, potted, sit up there for their confabulation about human skeletons; the boys stand tiptoe on it to see the races through the window; Christy – snared by the rope – leaps atop it, and is then pulled down, toppling the table with a loud crash. The crane beside the fire is like a balance beam for dancers; the actors hang and twirl on it. The rope brought to capture Christy is thick and long enough to go right across the whole stage; four men pull on one end, while Christy hangs on the other, with his ankles crossed around a table leg: it is a tour de force in the miming of strain. The action is wild and athletic, at many levels, and all across the stage area. The stage sees about as much physical activity in two hours as a rugby pitch.

The rhythms of Synge's dialogue are so lovely and so regular that they can produce uniformity from character to character, and an evenness of pace that is soporific. For this production, each sentence in a speech, and each phrase within a sentence, has evidently been examined with intelligence in rehearsal. The actors address each bit on its own, so the speeches have a rugged movement in congruence with the emotion. The actors make no effort to speak harmoniously in one accent, such as that of Mayo; each does what comes easily to that actor,[1] and this also reduces the effect of artificiality, which threatens any production of the play.

Overall, it seemed to me that Garry Hynes learned something since her 1982 production of *The Playboy* from the playwrights she directed in the 1990s, all of whom were heavily influenced by Synge: Marina Carr, Martin McDonagh, and John B. Keane. Hynes gives her intelligence and love of theatrical art to each playwright she directs. That meant in the case of Carr heightening the force of Greek fatalities in a provincial Irish setting (*On Raftery's Hill*, 1999). In McDonagh, it meant pulling out all the stops in dramatizing gags about Irish violence, Irish drunkenness, and Irish mean-mindedness (*Leenane Trilogy*, 1997). Returning to John B. Keane, Hynes found something others

---

[1] Only Frank O'Sullivan as Old Mahon seemed to me to speak with a pronouncedly western accent, and the Mahons are supposed to have come from Munster. Christy's accent is nothing like that of his father.

had not: Hieronymus Bosch and Pieter Brueghel, a social satire of rural life that is fantastic, grotesque, and profound (*Sive*, 2002; *Sharon's Grave*, 2003). Now in 2004, through a sort of feedback loop in the Syngean tradition of Irish drama, *The Playboy* manifests the traits of these more recent playwrights and productions. Their radical and postmodern aestheticizations of Irish rural life inspire a non-naturalist and almost 19th century melodramatic extravaganza. We do not for a moment imagine that we are getting a true account of life on the Erris Penisula in 1900; we witness a literary carnival of cartoons. Is this right? Is this good?

Those do not seem the right questions to me. The interpretation is certainly interesting, and there was no point in repeating the manky, angry style of the 1980s Druid *Playboy*, even if that interpretation was unanimously applauded by young audiences tired of romantic illusions about an Ireland that had been left behind economically by modern Europe. One effect of the new version is to reignite quarrels – though perhaps not as publicly as a century ago – about art and representation in Synge's plays. The old charge of 'hideous paddywhackery' is actually invited by the new production style. That may be a good thing. 'It is better to have the row we had last night', Synge wrote to Molly Allgood on 27 January 1907, 'than to have your play fizzling out in half-hearted applause.' [2]

---

2 Ann Saddlemyer, ed., *Letters to Molly* (Belknap Press, Harvard: Cambridge, 1971), p.88.

3 | Redesigning *The Playboy*

Nicholas Grene

'Parts of it are, or are meant to be, extravagant comedy,' Synge conceded in an uneasily worded letter to *The Irish Times* trying to retract his description of *The Playboy* as an extravaganza in the immediate wake of the riots. Not just parts of it in Garry Hynes's new Druid production, but almost all of it: physically extravagant, grotesque black comedy. Hynes, who in the 1980s rescued the play from a long tradition of comfortable comic playing by earthing it in a visually and emotionally realized style, has elected to go in exactly the opposite direction. Instead of the meticulously observed dirty realism of the shebeen, the Sacred Heart matched with the Gold Flake ad, there is an Irish cottage as Samuel Lover might have drawn it: dirt floor, high walls with roughly textured dark-green plaster rising up to a flat wooden ceiling, the free-standing fire in the centre of the room venting smoke through a hole in the roof. The costumes are equally tuned to the nineteenth-century style, top-hat and white muttonchop whiskers for Michael James, a black swallowtail coat offered to Christy by the trembling Shawn in Act Two. The physical postures are straight out of *Punch*: Gary Lydon's Shawn Keogh all cringe and crouch, the Mutt and Jeff partnership of the gangling Chris O'Dowd as Jimmy Farrell and the diminutive David Pearse as Philly O'Cullen. The somersaulting acrobatics of Cillian Murphy's Christy in the fight scene with his father (Frank O'Sullivan), the beautifully composed groupings of the onlookers in their shawls and ragged finery, would have won the approval of Dion Boucicault.

Hynes's realist *Playboy* was one of her landmark productions with Druid. But she is a director who never shirks big theatrical effects, and is prepared to work seriously with the melodramatic style. That was what made her production of John B. Keane's *Sharon's Grave* (Druid 2003) so powerful. It is not a great play, full of stagey handwringing and a histrionic pseudopoetry. But Hynes did not try to cover up its weaknesses; she played them as if they were strengths and, with the help of some outstanding performances from her actors, turned the play into a theatrical tour de force.

Here she directs Synge as if he were John B. Keane, or even more as if he were Martin McDonagh. She has wholly redesigned the play in this heightened, stylized, caricature style. There is hardly a straight back or a still upright posture held through the whole show. Widow Quin (Aisling O'Sullivan), sporting a scar on her left cheek perhaps acquired in her last terminal fight with her dead husband, the ewe-maiming Marcus Quin, leans forward, hands perpetually in pockets, like a long bird of prey. The courtship scenes between Christy and Pegeen (Anne-Marie Duff) are a choreographed ballet of bobbing and weaving, ducking and shuffling. The physical comedy is often splendidly inventive. In the opening scene of Act Three, the dead drunk Philly and Jimmy lying in intimate companionship stretched out on the table are just agreeing that Old Mahon's corpse 'should be rotten by now', when the undead Old Mahon appears at the high up window to block out the sunlight from them. They stare owlishly at their hands, baffled as to why they are suddenly in shadow, oblivious of the the lurking figure above. Never has the mule race watched from the window been put to better comic use as the three tall figures of Widow Quin, Jimmy and Old Mahon aloft on a bench telegraph back the progress of the race to the vertically challenged Philly, stuck on the table behind them.

Hynes has always had a director's eye for the tiny textual detail that can provide a production motif. In her earlier *Playboy* it was Widow Quin's line about Pegeen 'itching and scratching' realized by Brid Brennan's business during the opening letterwriting. (Anne-Marie Duff did give one slight scratch to the back of her neck as though in tribute to the earlier performance.) This time round Hynes has picked up on Pegeen's pub security: 'isn't herself the divil's daughter for locking?' complains Philly on his first entrance in Act Three, desperate in his need for a hair of the dog in the wake of Kate Cassidy's wake. This yields chains everywhere in the current production, long chains not only on the cupboards where the bottles are stored, but holding down the barrel of porter, chaining to the floor the table that serves as bar and much else. It is to this chain that Christy attaches himself when the men try to pull him out to be lynched. The practical usefulness is obvious, making believable Christy's capacity to resist the tugging of a whole tug-o'-war team trying to drag him out the door. But beyond that the implication is clear. These Mayo people would steal anything, even a large wooden table, if it were not chained down.

If the Abbey audience rioted at the original production in 1907, they might have torn the theatre apart if they had seen this 2004 version. This is the caricatured stage Irishry the national theatre movement had pledged itself to banish, drunks and dunderheads, clods and clowns. It is some sort of measure of where we are now nearly 100 years on that the Galway audience and the Dublin audience on the nights I saw it (Town Hall, Galway 13 February, Gaiety, Dublin 26 February) gave every sign of loving it. We can now afford to laugh heartily at this broadly grotesque version of ourselves. Indeed it is not a version of ourselves at all; it is an exercise in period pastiche. The actors can play the gags and the pratfalls for all they are worth – the twenty-first century Irish have no reason to think they are being mocked.

There is a loss, though, in this way of playing it, a loss of depth and emotional substance. Cillian Murphy is charming from start to finish, a charming chimp when he first enters, shoulders hunched up, arms swinging, timid face to one side peeping out from under the black hair. He manages the lines with real skill; it is a lovely voice with the break into a husky underside making it all the more winning. But there is no possibility of building a character within the director's chosen mannered style. The closest the production comes to a moment of emotional depth is his Act Two scene with Widow Quin. With Aisling O'Sullivan sitting back on the settle by the stage right wall, and most of the stage separating her from Christy kneeling behind a chair by the fire, and pauses where nothing can be heard but the tick of the wall-mounted clock's pendulum, there is the poignant glimpse of a possible connection between them that the scene demands. But the relationship between the winsome Christy and a pretty Pegeen is no more than a donné of the plot in this version.

I said in my 'Two London *Playboys*' essay that the difficult dilemma for any director of the play is to find a style to combine realism with the stylization that the language makes necessary. This time Hynes has jettisoned the realism altogether, ridden roughshod over the lyricism, and given full throttle to the grotesquerie. It's one way to go. And given the history of her previous productions, maybe it was the way she had to go. The audiences seem to be loving it; it's at the very least a good night out. But for me it adds nothing to our sense of what the play is and what it says. At the roundtable discussion of the production in Galway on 14 February several of the participants found the production disturbing as well as entertaining, politically challenging as well as visually satisfying. I cannot say that I agreed with them.

4 | Poetry, Romance, Clay, Worms

John P. Harrington

Nearly thirty years before she became widely known as a high literary modernist, Djuna Barnes was writing newspaper reviews for mainstream New York newspapers such as the *Morning Telegraph*. It might surprise readers of her novel *Nightwood*, or the famous introduction to it by T. S. Eliot, that one of her favourite subjects was John Millington Synge. In 1917, for the Sunday magazine of the *Telegraph*, Barnes wrote a feature called 'The Songs of Synge' that very accurately and somewhat inadvertently articulates some of the particular powers of the Druid production of *The Playboy of the Western World* as seen at Town Hall Theatre in February, 2004.

Like some other Greenwich Village artists at the time, Barnes was infatuated with Synge's *Riders to the Sea* and baffled both by *Playboy* and the angry Irish-American response to it. In her writing on Synge, Barnes celebrated the beauty of Synge's stage language. She did so in stereotypical, sentimental terms: 'He was a harp on which the sorrows and the great strifes played.' However, she did recognize the difference between *Playboy* and Synge's other plays. In *Playboy*, Synge 'realized that grim brutality and frankness are one, the upper lip is romance, but the under is irony, and he knew "There is no timber that has not strong roots among the clay and worms." '

Unfortunately, the immediate impact of Synge on Barnes was 'the upper lip', romance, and she wrote and had staged a series of embarrassing one-acts more like Dunsany than Synge; these included a mermaid tale called 'Kurzy of the Sea'. Much later, in *Nightwood*, she found the lower lip of irony and brutality and frankness. These darker dimensions are the quality of *Playboy* that counterbalances Synge's romanticism and separates, at least in degree, the current Druid production of *Playboy* from the company's two earlier productions in 1975 and 1982.

Much has been made of the company's initial studies for the production in Geesala, County Mayo. The *New York Times* did a feature on the workshop that was bylined Geesala and printed, of course, on St. Patrick's Day. But this wonderful production has much more to do with claustrophobic, dark, box-like spaces than with limitless horizons. The darkness of the opening scene is a radical revision of the play as customarily produced. As the play proceeds, bolts of light occasionally penetrate the space from windows and doors left and right. Geesala vistas are not part of the gloomy visual vocabulary of this production. They are part of the offstage world, presumably a more jovial one, that includes Kate Cassidy's wake and donkey races on the beach. The set we see instead is a deep gloom, with little reference to a country public-house; the direct reference is to a black box studio that Christy Mahon brightens by his presence and darkens with his exit.

Thomas Kilroy, Fintan O'Toole, and many others have written about how text has reigned supreme in many Irish productions. This production, which is seeking not merely to revive *Playboy* but to revise it, diminishes text and its invitation to the kind of 'Synge-song' admired by Djuna Barnes. With poetry in decline in this vision of the play, another focus must rise to replace it. For this *Playboy* the programme introduces the Druid production staff – director, designer, lighter, movement coach, costumer, sound designer – before the cast page. Among the many effective moments in the production are some that are nearly silent and communicate through light and movement and non-textual sounds. When Philly O'Cullen (David Pearse) and Jimmy Farrell (Chris O'Dowd) return drunk from the wake, they stand in place clinging to a vertical bar for support. Very dissimilar physically, the actors play off each other's posture while weaving in place, silently, at centre stage, for a long interlude. It is a grim image, of alcohol and dependence, and a powerfully silent one. The scene is particularly impressive because this new staging revises a moment of the play that especially lends itself to stage Irishman mugging and hilarity.

All the cast contribute to this newer vision of the play's brutality as counterbalance to its familiar romance. Both Widow Quin (Aisling O'Sullivan) and Old Mahon (Frank O'Sullivan) are cast younger than usual. That allows them to create more physical roles than is usual for the parts. It also gives a rather desperate quality to their efforts to secure some future a little less bleak than their present prospects. Michael James Flaherty (Eamon Morrissey) and the three young women (played by Sonya Kelly, Simone Kirby, and Gillian McCarthy) are all costumed and directed to be very rural, very backward, and very needy without any of the customary ingratiating charm.

Against this cast, and on a dimly lit dirt floor, Pegeen Mike (Anne-Marie Duff) and Christy Mahon (Cillian Murphy) are able in their love scenes to spin a web of lovely words that is heightened by contrast with the broader scene. Because of these roles and these performances, the production does not lack for romance. But here romance seems more doomed than it might in other settings. While Widow Quin and Old Mahon seem cast younger than usual, Pegeen and Christy seem cast smaller than usual. Duff and Murphy are certainly outweighed by anyone else on the stage, and, like many film actors, they appear to be small and perfectly formed. This gives them the physical capacity to swell as their confidence grows and then, in Pegeen's case, to physically communicate emotional deflation when prospects for change disappear.

It is interesting to consider this Druid production against two of its other great recent successes – Martin McDonagh's *The Beauty Queen of Leenane* and Tom Murphy's *Bailegangaire.* The McDonagh and Murphy plays also deromanticize some myths of the West and position small groups in small houses against dark and dreary landscapes once thought to be pastoral ideals. McDonagh and Murphy, of course, construct action from a far less poetic idiom than Synge. In McDonagh's *Beauty Queen* the forces frustrating characters are popular culture and the uniformity its invasion represents. In Murphy's *Bailegangaire*, the exterior forces eroding the home have to do with generational changes and consumerism supplanting oral culture. In both cases, the villain appears to be that old devil modernity. By contrast, Synge's *Playboy* finds no easy excuse in time for its analysis of desire and fear, of that great contrast between the gallous story and the dirty deed, and of personal victories and failures. In retrospect, it is the play from the beginning of the twentieth century, and the one that has come to seem most traditional and most elating in performance, that is harshest in its study of individual cowardice.

The new Druid production of *Playboy* makes that harsher quality of Synge's play more visible and so renews a text limited by familiarity and repetition. It is not, however, a simple inversion of expectations to make a gallous story dirty. It is, rather, a restoration of that kind of balance cited long ago by Djuna Barnes: the upper lip of romance and the lower one of brutality. The latter, a part of the story not always welcome, has to do with the clay and the worms. Almost a century earlier, in January, 1907, Joseph Holloway, that prolific Abbey diarist, angrily denounced Synge's *Playboy* in a famous passage about how it was the product of 'a morbid, unhealthy mind ever seeking on the dunghill of life for the nastiness that lies concealed there'. The new Druid production directed by Garry Hynes reminds us that Holloway was right. What he called 'dunghill' and Djuna Barnes called 'clay and worms' is in fact an essential counterpart of Synge's play to its poetry and beauty.

5 | Gallous Stories and Dirty Deeds

Mary C. King

The launch of the Druid cycle of Synge's works with a new performance of *The Playboy of the Western World* directed by Garry Hynes has inaugurated a project overdue in Ireland. Although all of his plays received excellent broadcast performances on Radio Éireann through October 1999, together with introductory talks and readings from the prose and poetry, to mark the ninetieth anniversary of his death, the Druid venture will offer the first opportunity to see each of the dramas on-stage, directed by the same director and performed by the same company.[1] Hynes intends to make it possible for an audience to see all of the plays over two or three days. Synge's plays lend themselves to such a venture because of their limited number and relative homogeneity. With this project comes the inviting prospect of revaluating his status as a key figure in the Irish drama of Europe.

New approaches to Synge have been developing apace over recent years in the academic world as well as in the theatre. We

---

Quotations from The Playboy of the Western World are from J. M. Synge, Collected Works: Volume IV, Plays Book II, ed. Ann Saddlemyer (London: Oxford University Press, 1968). Page references are given in the text.

[1] The RTE Radio One broadcasts were a mixture of new and archive materials. Each play was accompanied by a pre- or post-drama talk. The series included a version of *When the Moon Has Set.*

now know more than ever about the dramatist himself, his social, cultural, and political background, his relationships to the National Theatre movement that he helped found, and the history, performance, and reception of his plays.[2] Synge did not repeat Yeats's indictment that the audience by protesting noisily about *The Playboy* had disgraced themselves. On the contrary, he welcomed controversy, writing to his Catholic fiancée, the Abbey actress Molly Allgood, 'Now we'll be talked about. We're an event in the history of the Abbey stage.'[3] He wanted his plays to disturb and provoke as well as entertain. Garry Hynes has long maintained that there is a dark and disturbing side to Synge's comic world.[4] Druid's production of *The Playboy* evokes this darkness, projecting at the outset a sense of profound social disturbance. This production encourages audiences to look afresh at what has become the archetype of the west of Ireland comic peasant play.

The Druid *Playboy* takes place in a set that emphasizes the isolation of the 'interior' Western world from the hyperactivity of a mad, turbulent, alcoholic, and infinitely extendable 'outside' Western world. The restless movement between these worlds, the repeated dramatic rhythm of the eruptions of the one into

---

2 Several important studies of Synge, his writings and his life have appeared recently. These include W. J. McCormack's two major books of political biography, *Fool of the Family: A Life of J. M. Synge* (London: Weidenfeld & Nicolson, 2000); and *The Silence of Barbara Synge* (Manchester and New York: Manchester University Press, 2003). See also the excellent chapters on Synge in Lionel Pilkington, *Theatre and the State in Twentieth-Century Ireland* (London and New York: Routledge, 2001); Ronan McDonald,*Tragedy and Irish Literature: Synge, O'Casey, Beckett.* Basingstoke and New York: Palgrave, 2002; and Ben Levitas, *The Theatre of Nation: Irish Drama and Cultural Nationalism, 1860 – 1916* (Oxford: Clarendon Press, 2002).

3 See Christopher Morash's chapter, 'All Playboys Now: The Audience and the Riot' in Nicholas Grene, ed., *Interpreting Synge: Essays from the Synge Summer School, 1991 – 2000.* (Dublin: The Lilliput Press, 2000).

4 See Cathy Leeney's interview with Garry Hynes in Lilian Chambers, Ger FitzGibbon and Eamonn Jordan eds, *Theatre Talk: Voices of Irish Theatre Practitioners* (Dublin: Carysfort Press, 2001).

the other, is intimately related to the psychic drama of the play. This power of disturbance is also carried in the language, in the stylistic interrogation of the gap between word and deed, and in the tensions between excess, including sexual excess, and paralysis, decay, and impotence. The shebeen in which all three acts are set should be the place where the men drink, but one of the many pregnant paradoxes of Synge's play is that, apart from Christy's rudely interrupted marriage binge with the Widow Quin, it is not. The alcohol-soaked menfolk come in drunk from the Western World outside, having waked and buried a woman and retched over her grave.[5] The Druid shebeen could be part of a Union, a prison, or a decaying Gothic Big House. High, dark metallic walls surround the stage. Covered with verdigris, they seem to ooze a slimy rust of neglect. The doors, left of stage leading outside, and back right, to the bedroom, are scarcely visible until they are opened. A high window, side right, is shuttered when the curtain rises on Pegeen.

The Pegeen Mike of this Act One could be Sister Eileen from *When the Moon Has Set.* It would be interesting to see that drama played in an adaptation of this set, with Anne-Marie Duff as Eileen. Changes to rustic furniture and earth floor could easily suggest the decaying country house with a turf fire low in the fireplace that Synge requests for his first play. There would be little need to alter greatly the gibbet-like fire, with its

---

[5] There are several 'off-stage' dead women in Synge's play. They include Christy's mother, Pegeen's mother, Kate Cassidy, and the women after whom The Stooks of the Dead Women are named. Bridie Quin has researched carefully the local history of areas mentioned in the play and she has discovered that 'this refers to a terrible drowning, where several women, all dressed in green, were found in a boat which had broken up in a storm ... on the Kerry coast.' Synge has transferred the Stooks to Mayo, but Christy claims to have murdered his da in Kerry. See *Irish Times*, Saturday, 7 February 2004, Weekend Review, p.7.

long hanging bar, that smoulders back centre stage throughout the performance, waiting to be slowly and purposefully blown into vengeful heat in Act Three by a despairingly regressive Pegeen. The choice of piano music, one of Dvorak's light *Humoresques*, that prepares us for the raising of the Druid curtain, even suggests a Victorian parlour scene. It subtly evokes very different expectations from those raised by the Irish folk music played by The Chieftains that introduced the London National Theatre production that opened at the Old Vic in 1975 before transferring in the following year to the South Bank. Dressed in a faded yellow Victorian lady's gown, Duff's Pegeen moves with constrained, restless boredom about small domestic tasks before sitting sideways at the large table. This table takes on a character role of its own as the play develops, acting as a platform for the stage audience relaying to the theatre audience Christy's exploits at the races and restored to its place by Shawn Keogh with the vindictive resounding thud of restored domestic proprieties when Christy has finally departed.

Each act of *Playboy* begins with a listing, a recursive structuring device that requires on each occasion careful attention.[6] Marie-Ann Duff writes and speaks her list with pauses and glances that question the coincidence of speech with writing – a small but important touch in a play that explores the gap between stories and deeds. A subtle blend of laconic dreaming alternates with fierce digging of pen into paper as she moves from the female items for her trousseau to the order for them to be sent with three barrels of porter. There is no sense of excitement about her forthcoming nuptials, suggesting a yawning chasm between the event and her enthusiasm for it. The repressed sexuality of the woman and her proud sense of identity are nicely caught by the fiery inflection on boots with *brassy eyes* and the combination of vocal emphasis, thoughtful looking up and manual flourish with which she signs her full first name and

---

6 See McCormack's comparison of these lists to lists in Asenath Nicholson's *Annals of the Famine in Ireland*, in *Fool*, pp.246–7.

patronymic, *Margaret Flaherty*. This is the first and last time she is accorded that formal dignity and she confers it on her *solitary* self.

Duff's Pegeen Mike is played throughout with an intelligent combination of watchful reserve, introverted energy, and explosive anger. She quickly establishes herself as a woman who must look to her own survival in a world of feckless and neglectful men. She will not easily yield to fine words, even though desirable men are scarce and her soul starved. Duff's interpretation of the role suggests something of the watchful, interrogative *ressentiment* of an Irish Hedda Gabler.[7] Her sudden, angry taking the butt of a broom to Christy in Act One and fierce dismissal of the village girls and the Widow Quin in Act Two endorse the Widow's judicious warning to Christy that life with this Pegeen will not be all poetry talk. Her well-paced account of her forensic investigation of what the newspapers might or might not have to say about Christy's crime and her enactment of how he might hang for it is delivered with an accompanying verbal sadism that anticipates her final act of treachery when she burns Christy's leg with a sod of turf. This Pegeen rises from a low key, interrogative, almost ironic note to the operatic ecstasy of her duet with Christy's poetry-talk in Act Two, communicating a repressed, disappointed, even angry eroticism. That eroticism, the red thread of sex that Synge claimed to have restored to Irish drama, survives in the playing of Sarah Tansey, Susan Brady, and Honor Blake as nubile, exuberant, sensation-hungry teenagers on the cusp of expectant womanhood in a meagre world. Their choice of men is limited outside to cutthroat khakis, impoverished vagabonds and madmen and inside to maudlin alcoholics or repressed religious bigots like Shawn Keogh.

---

[7] Hedda Gabler tells Lövberg to die beautifully by her father's pistol. Like Pegeen, she does not want to face the realities of a dirty deed. She tells Judge Brack that all these gory details don't concern her.

Cillian Murphy's Christy has been criticized in one or two nit-seeking press reviews for his fine head of shiny, shampooed hair, but I did not find this disruptive of the integrity and discipline of Hynes's over-all direction. His locks are well hidden initially under his cap and their showing forth is of a piece with his delighted discovery of his fine self in the mirror. Hair plays an interesting part in the imagery and action of *The Well of the Saints,* and it scarcely damages the playboy to show a bit of his crowning glory in this production! Murphy's handling of the mirror episode is totally credible in its choreography and control, as is the pacing of his response to the wonderfully suggestive offering of gifts from the village girls. His self-scrutiny as new and admiring others have begun to see him is a part of his multipart journey towards establishing a first person singular identity objectively, from within and over against a pathologically diseased patriarchal society that admires him for his rebellion against it and then redeploys words and blows to beat his hard-won identity out of him.

On the opening night, the timorous, slow entry of Christy round the door and his advancement into the shebeen as the silent on-stage audience gaze with dark wary reflection on his wariness, kept the theatre audience suspended in the disquieted quiet essential for any production that works against the grain of the easy laughter that too often fatally damages performances of the play at the first appearance of its hero. Synge's Christy has murdered his da to escape from abuse, beatings, drunkenness, perversion, and incestuous attempts to force him to marry his wet nurse. Murphy's initial defensive, sly terror at any movement towards him and his sudden collapses from confident boasting to cowering despair make him a disturbed and disturbing cousin to Patrick Galvin's raggy boy, and provides food for thought for a modern Irish audience.[8]

---

[8] The depth and extent of 'child abuse' in the *Playboy* is all too often overlooked. Hynes's production leaves us in no doubt as to what Christy has endured. Teatre Warszawa's production of *Festen*, based on Thomas Vinterberg's and Mogens Rukov's film and performed at the Abbey Theatre in January 2004 is a fascinating anatomy of the

The powerful presence, savagery, and physical and linguistic brutality of Eamonn Morrissey's Old Mahon, his wielding of stick, feet, curses, and humiliating language against Christy, leave no doubt that the trembling, terrorized playboy is a product and victim of real patriarchal violence. The same violence of the fathers has turned Shawn Keogh into a father-fearing, misogynistic, and sadistic opportunist. The initial counterparts, to use a Joycean term, between Christy and Shawn Keogh are pointed up in the play-text and are carried by much stage business. For instance, Christy dresses in Shawn's best (wedding) clothes in Act Two. The business of clothes, part of this drama's relentless playing with the playing of roles, is managed well throughout, including the cross-gender dressing of Christy in petticoats and his extrication of himself from these. The Druid decision to use Shawn's top hat and frock coat for Christy takes up nicely the gentrified Victorian theme initiated with Pegeen's dress and continued in the more tattered gentry costume of Michael James. Eamon Morrisey plays Pegeen's father as a fading, dissolute, and neglectful paterfamilias with a residual streak of sadism that he directs against Shawn, his prospective son-in-law, second cousin to Pegeen, and the most timorous, father-obsessed man in the public house. Perhaps there is an appropriate revenge in Shawn's carrying Michael back to the shebeen after the races, rather than supporting him, as Synge suggests. However, as a result the audience cannot hear Michael James's menacing and prophetic ballad about hanging. This is one of a series of leitmotivs of lynching, from Jimmy Farrell's hanging his dog to the noose that Pegeen places around Christy's neck at the end of the play. These men belong

---

pervasive pathology of abuse, and its collusiveness with fascism racism and misogyny, in bourgeois authoritarian and patriarchal western society. Many parallels of theme, technique, form and style with Synge's *Playboy* in this production were striking. The second part of Patrick Galvin's memoirs, *The Raggy Boy Trilogy* (Dublin: New Island Books, 2002), recently released as a major feature film starring Aidan Quinn, is a harrowing account of an Ireland that all but ate its young.

passionately to, and are fearful and easily cowed colonial subjects of, a legal, imperial patriarchy. Even though, or perhaps because, they live at the margins of Empire, they fear and sadistically enforce the long arm of the English Law. It is ultimately to this fear that Pegeen succumbs when she rejects Christy's last plea to free him and let him go as an outlawed Tom O'Bedlam 'eating muck and green weeds on the faces of the cliffs': 'And leave us to hang, is it, for a saucy liar, the like of you?' she retorts, '[*To* MEN.]Take him on out from this' (p. 169).

In this Druid production, great credit must go to the orchestration of the first act, which Garry Hynes saw as probably the greatest interpretative challenge to any contemporary director.[9] Gary Lydon's Shawn Keogh is a triumph of intelligent and empathetic role-playing. Posture, gesture, voice, and movement realize a sustained virtuoso interpretation of his crucial function, first as twin, then as foil, to Christy, but the connotations of the character go far beyond that. Shawneen is the product and apotheosis of the father-dominated, authority fearing and wielding, cringing and mercenary, sexually repressed moralizing spirit that is sapping the community's manhood and forcing its women to seek vicarious erotic satisfaction in gossip and press reports of sensations and atrocities. Lydon played him consistently as such, from his frantic wriggling out of the coat of a Christian man to his revived whingeing hope that he'll wed Pegeen when he recovers from the mad bite of his poetry-talking rival.

Christy's counting of the jugs and bottles that opens Act Two is part of the economics of *The Playboy*, part of the buying and bargaining theme that pervades the action. This reaches a recursive double climax of theme and variation when Shawn and Christy each tries to strike an almost identical compromising bargain with the Widow Quin in exchange for help in winning Pegeen. The Widow demands from Shawn 'the red

---

[9] Garry Hynes's response to a question at the Round Table Discussion, Druid Theatre, Galway, 14 February 2004.

cow you have and the mountainy ram, and the right of way across your rye-path, and a load of dung at Michaelmas, and turbary upon the western hill' (p.127) and from Christy she requires ' a right of way I want, and a mountainy ram and a load of dung at Michaelmas, the time that you'll be master here' (p.151). Cillian Murphy's shrewd stocktaking in Act One is suitably self-seeking, looking with presumptuous swiftness to the time when he will be master of the shebeen and of Pegeen Mike. His boastful, braces-pulling speech about this being 'a fine place to be my whole life talking out with swearing Christians in place of my old dogs and cat, and I stalking around, smoking my pipe and drinking my fill, and never a day's work but drawing a cork an odd time, or wiping a glass' is delivered from the added height of a chair (p.95). His calculating smugness made one ponder whether, in the end, he'd make a husband all that different from the mercenary Shawn Keogh. At the opening of Act Three, the table at which Pegeen wrote her order for her trousseau and the drink for the men provides the platform for the final listing device: Philly and Jimmy's rustic Hamlet-like exchange about the skulls ranged out like blue jugs in a cabin of Connaught. At this point there erupts into the play the Conradian darkness of violent racism alongside the ethnographical and imperialist predilection for collecting 'white skulls and black skulls and red skulls' and ranging them according to a pseudo-Darwinian hierarchy of racial types (p. 135). [10]

Chris O'Dowd's lanky, long-armed, and lugubrious Jimmy certainly incarnates the simianism attributed to the native Irish, with David Pearse's Philly as its complementary low-browed decadence. I felt uncomfortable, however, with this casting. The pair, too inebriated throughout, were especially distracting at the opening of Act Three. Their boozy clowning drew one's attention away from the dark comedy of the dialogue and the dramatic linking of Old Mahon's bloodied skull with those

---

[10] For an excellent detailed study of Synge and ethnography see Gregory Castle, *Modernism and the Celtic Revival*, (Cambridge: Cambridge University Press, 2001), chapter 3.

ranged out in cabinets in Dublin's Natural History Museum. As Bill McCormack pointed out in his Galway lecture, Pegeen's account in Act One of how 'Jimmy Farrell hanged his dog from the licence and had it screeching and wriggling three hours at the butt of a string' is one of the stories without a gap between it and the dirty deed, and, moreover, Jimmy is present onstage as she narrates it. For those prepared to follow Synge's prompts to move beyond the stage of the play to the wider Western world, during times of sectarian strife, and in the Mayo beyond the stage door, Protestants had a nasty habit of hanging dogs (read 'God' in reverse) outside Catholic homes, as a warning and a calculated blasphemy against their wearing of crucifixes hung with a figure of Jesus.

Aisling O'Sullivan has been widely acclaimed for her playing of the part of the Widow Quin in this production. She is from the start until almost the end the lynchpin, the centrifugal force, that holds in place the frenetic movement between extremes around a profoundly dark, still point in a turning world. Hynes has cast The Widow well, young and feisty enough to be a credible rival to Pegeen in Christy's affections, yet able to project with smouldering lonesomeness the hard experience wrung from the darker pleasures of eros and the sinister attractions of liebestod. O'Sullivan's Widow is well fitted to deal with the absent Father Reilly, the ecstatic and despairing Christy, the whingeing, calculating Shawn and the bullying and bragging Old Mahon, all of whom Synge thought of as possible husbands for her when he drafted the play. He also thought of making her the proud widow of a north of Ireland judge. O'Sullivan's Widow Quin is a triumph for Druid and a measure of the profound empathy with Synge that Hynes and her team have brought to bear on this production. Should Christy go with her, we wonder, would he become the servant of another hard master – the androgynous Widow smokes a pipe – or would he be the fire-side darling of the only woman strong enough to survive and thrive in the Western World beyond the shebeen? The Widow Quin is the great storyteller of the play who is well able to engineer transformations, encounters and escapes and who elicits from Old Mahon the ecstatic confession that he and his Western world are mad. The life she offers Christy does not differ much from the one Martin and Mary Doul choose at the end of *The Well of the Saints* and she is conspicuously absent from the vindictive group that gathers to torture Christy at the end, having gone by the back door to call the doctor. Perhaps O'Sullivan will reappear as Mary Doul in the Druid production of *The Well*, Synge's greatest and least appreciated play. I await that event in the Druid-Synge Cycle with great hopes for another major production as sensitive to Synge's genius as this 2004 *Playboy*.

6 | Notes from the Borderland

Bill Mc Cormack

> The shallow depression in the west of these islands is likely to move slowly in an easterly direction. There are no indications of any great change in the barometrical situation.
> (Liza Doolittle in G.B. Shaw, *Pygmalion*, 1912)

Though stage-sets are the first element of any production to affect the audience, they rarely have the impact achieved in the new Druid production of Synge's *The Playboy of the Western World.* Gone are the folksy props which imply a traditional cottage interior. Gone is the view of yellow corn or blue sea through window or open door in Act Two. Instead the lights come up on a vertiginous wall of mottled, metallic grey-green, its texture oily or watery like the inside of a fuel tank. The sub-industrial tonalities are underlined by the vertical pillar or girder near-centre-stage, beside the fire. Other items soften the blow – a sturdy table big enough to serve as a stage-on-the-stage, and an upholstered chair suggesting different previous ownership. But the unavoidable emotional impact is of improvised living space, at once marginalized and exposed. Think of the bad lands in Dakota; think of the as-yet-not-Mad Mulrannies and they heading west to California; think galvanized.

A good production of a great play can afford to disclose weak links in the plot or underdeveloped relations between formidable characters. Against the iron backdrop of Francis O'Connor (design) and Davy Cunningham (lighting), Pegeen

Mike commences to write out her shopping list, items of her trousseau plus drink. Perhaps Anne-Marie Duff delivered her opening lines a shade too fast, for in every respect this production rightly slows the pace of Synge's dialogue to admit its menace. Yet the discrepancy brought me to consider what the relationship between Pegeen and her father is. She runs the business, she is about to be married, is 'about twenty years' old, evidently an only child. He ruins the business, is a widower and prematurely aged. The total and unremarked absence of a mother/wife never struck me so forcibly in any production I had previously seen.

In an informal seminar, Garry Hynes explained the upholstered chair as her notion of what the mother had brought to the family, a relic of old decency now pushed round the earthen floor. If Mrs Flaherty has been dead some time, what has been the state of things between father and daughter? It is a legitimate question, not of the 'How Many Children Suckled Lady Macbeth?' kind. Pegeen is to marry a man of whom her father condescendingly approves though, at the same time, the Holy Father has yet to grant a dispensation. More urgently Michael James is on his way to a wake, recurrent reminder of the end his wife has already made and which we will all make. Pegeen never addresses him as Father, she calls him Michael James to his face. Her most articulate account of their relationship is even-handed and empty-handed:

> If I am a queer daughter, it's a queer father'd be leaving me lonesome these twelve hours of dark, and I piling the turf with the dogs barking, and the calves mooing, and my own teeth rattling with the fear.

Shawn Keogh is her pathetic saviour in waiting. Of all the men heard or heard of in the play, only he is explicitly related to a place-name, though there are place-names a-plenty to be sure. Once or twice he is 'Shawn Keogh of Kilakeen'. It is a nondescript line, yet a puzzling one. The Widow Quin's attitude is mocking, almost contemptuous, and it may be that she ironically underscores his complacent pride in proprietorship by invoking the townland or farmland name he claims as his own.

This may be squireen ambition to ape 'Johnston of Ballykilbeg' or 'The Byrnes of Cloneen', social eminence not only beyond Keogh's personal reach but lost in the welter of land legislation which is producing Keogh's type. Neither Jimmy Farrell nor Philly O'Cullen has this nominal attachment: instead, in this visually stunning production, they appear like displaced figures in physical scale and verbal performance. Pegeen worries about 'the loosèd khaki cut-throats, or the walking dead' roving the roads while Philly and Jimmy mimic such grotesques in her kitchen. Like the galvanized interior of a 'country public house or shebeen, very rough and untidy', presence and appearance conflict in these two figures. At the opening of Act Three, the director brilliantly exploits the apparent height of one and the shortness of the other. The pair are sitting or lolling drunkenly on the sturdy table, discussing evidences of death. Philly recalls, 'when I was a young lad, there was a graveyard beyond the house with the remnants of a man who had thighs as long as your arm' – and Jimmy glances anxiously at the long thigh of Philly beside him. Who, indeed, are the walking dead in *The Playboy of the Western World*?

There is a symmetry of unease here. Mrs Flaherty is absent presumed dead, Jimmy and Philly are present and presumed alive. Definition of the line which makes this distinction is central to the play – has Christy killed his Da or not? If the community into which the young man arrives is strongly marked by inanition, vacuity, inactivity, from what kind of place (community, or other) has he come? Early audiences were in no doubt as to the exact setting, for they took references to North Connacht and 'the County Mayo' seriously, even literally. For their benefit, the text also provides Christy with a provenance through references to stories you might read 'in any little paper of a Munster town', and through supportive allusions to Kerry, Limerick and Clare. Christy, we are to believe, is from the south-west of Ireland. Geographically, culturally and linguistically, he has crossed significant lines or boundaries to reach 'this place' as the local men refer to it on their first gathering in the shebeen. When Christy enters some minutes later, he emphasizes the importance of exact but unnamed location when he delivers the accepted salutation, 'God save all here'.

Probing his identity, the men (led by Michael James Flaherty) progressively focus on whom it may be Christy has killed – bailiff, agent or landlord. They make no enquiry about his regional origins because, as their behaviour indicates, it is as well not to know too much. In so far as their inquiries can be classified as 'social', they are socio-pathological. What they want to know is his status in the lists of approved killing, not his place of birth or mode of living. On this detail, the Peacock Theatre production of 2001 opted most effectively to cast Jimmy and Philly as trench-coated look-out men at an interrogation, what Marx in another context called 'murderous dreamers on street corners'. When Christy admits that he has 'killed' his father, the practical consequence soon is that Michael James can in good conscience leave his daughter and go to the wake. That is, he too is dispatched by Christy.

Seen in this light, the play takes on a stronger resemblance to Freudian paradigms than has generally been conceded by critics. As literary texts cannot *per se* be psychoanalysed, the argument inevitably swings back to concentrate on the playwright. From the outset, *The Playboy of the Western World* was closely associated with its author's life. It was well-known that Synge wrote the part of Pegeen Mike for the actress with whom he was in love. Consequently a play, opening with a scene in which the character played by Molly Allgood anticipates her marriage, leaves itself open to interpretation in terms of their lives, Synge's and Allgood's. It was less well-known, but soon evident to those close to him, that *The Playboy* would be his last completed work. It stands as his artistic confrontation with death, or – Yeats might say – as an antithetical confrontation with death.

These factors may illuminate the under-developed relationship between Pegeen and Michael James already noted. In a rudimentary sense, neither Molly nor John Synge had grown up in the company of a father: the relationship was one that author and actress were personally unfamiliar with. It is, I realize, near-treasonable to suggest that a masterpiece of Irish literature is marred by such crudely circumstantial and external factors, but one must acknowledge again the dramatic evidence. At no point in the tumultuous action, in the rapid ebb-and-flow of her emotions, does Pegeen refer to her father either for guidance in the present or for explanation of the past. As for his attitude towards her, the only instance of powerful feeling occurs in the final act when the question of her marriage is urgently raised.

The urgency itself is questionable in terms of dramatic construction. Michael James has just returned from Kate Cassidy's wake to which he had departed at the close of Act One. His absence from the significant action of the middle act should be noted. The wake has been followed by the local sports at which we can assume Michael James ran a hair of the dog to ground. Despite these prolonged indulgences, he suddenly announces in Act Three that he is 'after getting the gilded dispensation this day to wed them [Pegeen and Shawn] now'. Previously the matter had been in the hands of Father Reilly. Suddenly, the father is in charge, determined to marry off his daughter *now*. The moment turns on his revised opinion of Christy, a prize-winning hero at the local sports.

From the instant of his arrival on stage, Michael James evinces jovial hostility towards the triumphant intruder. 'Wasn't it a shame I didn't bring you along with me to Kate Cassidy's wake ... ?' Such a decision would of course have left Pegeen alone, her teeth 'rattling with the fear'. It would have initiated Christy into self-destructive drinking, incapacitating him for the sports. But that is all supposing. Allowing just four words of acknowledgement by Christy, Michael James proceeds to call him 'a lousy schemer' for failing to deliver his dead father, thus frustrating the need for another wake. That may be cheery enough, for the playboy ('a hardened slayer') is slapped on the back. The father moves on rapidly to the dispensation and, with it, implications of his own relationship to the bride. 'It'll be a poor thing for the household man where you go sniffing for a female wife; and [*pointing to* SHAWN] look beyond at that shy decent Christian I have chosen for my daughter's hand ... ' In this way, Michael James will rid himself of the man who aided and abetted his absence at the wake.

All four characterizations deserve attention. Instead of pater familias, head of the family or some such title of authority, Michael James chooses to use a neologism 'the household man' for his own equivalent in any place where Christy might wed. Though it might tenuously be treated as a translation of *fear an tigh* [literally, man of the house] 'the household man' carries no air of power or authority, conveying little beyond an implication of solitariness. Far more potent is the phrase 'sniffing for a female ...' Compared to the innocuous 'shift' of which so much is reported, this olfactory tribute to the lures and lunges of sexual union should in itself have brought the house down. The locus of so potent a realization of sex is not indicated with entire clarity. Is Christy primarily detected as one likely to sniff? Alternatively, is Pegeen accused of being keenly redolent, inviting of his attentions? Or, additionally, is Michael James not revealed as a man who, in relation to his daughter, is acutely aware of sexual attraction in its most intimate signals? In this last connection, his preference for the non-descript term might be read as self-effacing. One way or another, a shy, decent Christian would have no nose for this bouquet, and so is preferred as Pegeen's household man.

No minute-by-minute account of the riots in 1907 has identified the exact prompt to uproar. On the contrary, there is a gathering consensus that trouble was brewing even before the opening night, and that malcontents in the audience were murmuring well before the retrospectively acknowledged cue-word. It is certainly worth considering the word 'shift' as simply Lady Gregory's preferred short-hand for an aspect of Synge's material she found difficult to discuss, especially in a telegram. Michael James's forthright enunciation of the 'must' in human sexual drives is not the only passage in the play to outstrip the shift in offensiveness. Pegeen's scornful retort to the Widow Quin in their first encounter contains matter which mixes female biology with Catholic theology: 'Doesn't the world know you reared a black ram at your own breast, so that the Lord Bishop of Connaught felt the elements of a Christian, and he eating it after in a kidney stew?' This may be wild exaggeration ('a gallous story') but it violates propriety with suggestions of bestiality, second-degree cannibalism, and outrage to the sacraments. (In the Eucharist, the faithful eat the body of Christ – or lamb of god – after the *elements* – bread and wine – are transubstantiated.) Listening to the Druid production in February 2004, one felt that a desire to rush these lines robbed them of their offensiveness, the desire being its own tribute to the offence.

Even earlier and less luridly, the play exposed sexual practices and domestic irregularities to which no Irish audience had been exposed. Christy, explaining to Pegeen the circumstances in which he came to strike his father dead, denies the suggestion that the two of them had 'great tussling then':

> We had not then. It was a hard woman was come over the hill, and if he was always a crusty kind, when he'd a hard woman setting him on, not the devil himself or his four fathers could put up with him at all.

His repetition of her 'then' enacts the closeness already drawing them to each other, just as her 'tussling' opens out the emotional charge shared in fighting and love-making which the play later explores. But, in terms of characterization which the 1907 audience understood, the plain meaning of these lines was that Old Mahon was in the habit of casual co-habitation with a succession of women, these liaisons bringing violence on his son.

Máire nic Shiubhlaigh's view that *The Playboy* was Synge's retaliation on an audience which jibbed at *In the Shadow of the Glen* and murmured against *The Well of the Saints* becomes all the more plausible as one listens closely to the dialogue. In the wake of the Druid production, I am inclined to revise my own opinion that the evidence of Mary Maguire (Mrs Padraic Colm) and others identifies the word 'shift' as the detonating offence: it can have been no more than the occasion for the release of feelings built up virtually from the moment Pegeen authorizes her own trousseau, suggestively ordering boots with 'lengthy heels on them and brassy eyes'. Clothes unmaketh the woman.

Pegeen's free-wheeling attitude to her future is not acquisitive but disruptive; she seeks not security but experience.

This venturesomeness marks her established relations with other characters. We might begin by wondering if, with Shawn Keogh in prospect as a mate, she does not signal the greater importance of ridding herself of Michael James, getting the Mike out of Pegeen Mike. Signal, it must be, for nothing verbal in the text requires such an interpretation. Relations between daughter and father are implicit which is close to saying they are repressed, as least textually. Quite the opposite situation arises in her confrontation with Christy. Their words enact the initial discerning, gradual desiring, and climactic realizing of mutual passion. The unconscious lie about slaying the father may lie behind the dialogue of young lovers, but eloquent, articulate dialogue there unquestionably is.

And yet one rich potency of language remains unheard in this discussion. How does Christy sound to his auditors when he utters the standard salutation, 'God save all here'? Synge's stage-directions indicate 'a small voice'. There is a gamut of considerations yet to be addressed. Does this small voice convey remote origins in the speaker, and/or class difference? Pegeen – for reasons deserving comment – thinks of Christy's as a 'quality' surname, and admires the smallness of his feet as further evidence of social distinction. Does the actor convey anything of these qualities when he enunciates his opening four words? Does he have a Munster accent or even, more particularly, a north Kerry accent? Smallness of voice may postpone the issue on stage, but should not rule it out of subsequent debate.

In the Saturday morning discussion in Galway which followed the opening of the Druid's new production, Garry Hynes discussed how *The Playboy* cannot be cast or directed nowadays with reference to the elaborate differences heard between Ballylongford and Erris. These were sharper in Synge's day than in 2004, just as the social and economic implications of voice, accent, speech and language were then coming into active play. Quite apart from the English Dean's discussion with Stephen Dedalus, Joyce's *Portrait* (1916) provides a wealth of evidence on this point through comment on occasional rural characters (Davin) and figures from the lower echelons of

Dublin society. In earlier productions, directors and actors felt some obligation towards literalism (or auralism) in this regard: Christy should not sound the same as Jimmy, Shawn or Michael James. For good and ill, audiences of diverse backgrounds are now ill-equipped to notice subtleties of rural intonation.

They would, however, detect a true Dub as readily as the Ascot crowd in 'My Fair Lady' spotted Liza Doolittle. Or a Belfastman. These exceptions may lack scientific proof but they indicate the fundamental divisions of Irish society which would soon be superimposed over the parish-and-barony music of idiom and dialect. Rural Ireland versus the city, six counties against twenty-six; these were to be the grand divisions, and remain so. Ironically, *The Playboy* in the 1920s becomes a vehicle on which the new order reconciles itself to a betrayed past, an abandoned hinterland. But when Synge was writing the play, these were the painfully emergent divisions. As a counterpoint to my unpatriotic suggestion that there are moments when interrelationship between characters is incompletely clarified, let me suggest that there are also some highly suggestive isolated verbal details.

The most obvious of these arises from Pegeen's comment on the playboy's names, revealed with all formality as Christopher Mahon. 'You should have had great people in your family, I'm thinking, with the little small feet you have, and you with a kind of a quality name, the kind of what you'd find on the great powers and potentates of France and Spain.' It is difficult to reconcile this with the relatively common names which he has given, though the earlier drafts shed light on the issue. Synge's editor, Ann Saddlemyer, reports that Christy in these gives 'a false name' which (after trial and error) becomes Simon Fitzhenry or Henry Fitzsimon. The trials and errors have their own interest as, for some brief moment in the composition of the play, Christy uses the names Mulvaney and Flaherty, the latter nominally relating him to Pegeen and Michael James. But the Norman-style names, Fitzsimon (not uncommon) and Fitzhenry (more unusual), justify Pegeen's allusion to a 'quality name' to be found on the potentates of Anglo-Normandy if not actual France. It is possible that, having opted for the name Christy Mahon, Synge neglected to modify Pegeen's response to the earlier names, or was happy to leave it as evidence of her romantic indulgence.

The second textual 'island' is distinguished by two features. It occurs in the only song heard in *The Playboy* and it names a place in Ulster. The relevant action follows Michael James's return drunk from the wake. He is heard off-stage: The jailor and the turnkey

> They quickly ran us down,
> And brought us as prisoners
> Once more to Cavan town.

To the best of my knowledge, nobody has identified this ballad in editing *The Playboy* or commenting thereon. Irish ballads are notoriously free with proper nouns, though Cavan is not a high scorer in the citation indexes. The county of Cavan, however, had certain few links with Mayo where the play is set. The Pratt family owned an estate (Cabra Castle) at Kingscourt in east Cavan, and another at Enniscoe in North Mayo; more to the point, the playwright's elder brother was land agent at Cabra Castle and occasional functionary for the Pratts in Mayo also. Edward Synge was employed to enforce payment of rents and to preside over the negotiation of leases; with the Land War raging, he devoted much energy and personal zeal to evicting resistant tenants in Mayo (and also in Wicklow where his relatives borrowed his expertise.)

Nobody pays the slightest attention to Michael James's singing, either as action or allusion. Shaking Christy 'drunkenly by the hand', he delivers a distinctly Catholic benediction, 'The blessing of God and the holy angels on your head, young fellow.' Christy employs or adopts a similar idiom. But elsewhere, in the play as completed by Synge and even more so in the drafts, there is evidence of a rival denominational practice. During the interrogation of Christy in Act One, Jimmy Farrell on two occasions makes reference to what would seem to be Protestant groups, while maintaining the tone of fantastical exaggeration which dominates the reception given the wandering youth. 'He'd beat Dan Davies' Circus or the holy missioners on the villainy of man.' And a few sentences later he asks, 'Did you marry three wives maybe? I'm told there's a sprinkling have done that among the holy Luthers of the preaching North.' These enquiries are richly indicative of the mutual dependence underpinning sectarian difference in Irish Edwardian times (and later). It is clear that the speaker is not affiliated to the missioners or the Luthers; each term is an improvisation which reaches towards a hearer who may know an accepted equivalent term. Do these questions of Jimmy's hint that Christy may be a Protestant or (at least) is suspected of being a Protestant?

The play-text, and Synge's drafts towards the final version, offer some supporting evidence of this hypothesis. The dramatist worked diligently to find the exact phrase he wanted, and the rejected alternative sometimes reveals a stronger presentation of religious conflict. For instance, 'the holy Luthers' had previously been 'the Orange of the north'. One of Pegeen's scornful dismissals of the Widow Quin originally compared her to 'Satan's ma'. Synge's most dedicated editor has suggested that phrases in Notebook 10 of the Trinity College Synge Manuscripts about 'a bloody souper saying "To hell with the Pope" ...' may have been intended for Christy's lips towards the end of Act One. The notorious blasphemies of the play, which contributed to the outrage in 1907, had sometimes accommodated more pious (if ironic) expressions of a bible-Protestant kind. Thus, Notebook 32 experimented with a curtain line for the first act which has Christy declare, 'Well the Almighty was wise surely and he writing in the Holy Scriptures it was a queer terrible world.' A draft of Act Two has Sally assure Christy that what she tells him is 'Bible truth', and the canonical text of the first act preserves a reference to the wanderings of Esau which would baffle all but Mrs Kathleen Synge's most devoted listeners.

This kind of evidence could be multiplied by citation of drafts and notebooks, though it is noteworthy that what one discovers through a careful reading of Ann Saddlemyer's annotations refers us back to draft material for Act One and (to a lesser extent) Act Two. In other words, this stratum of what might uncharitably be called The Sectarian Unconscious in

Synge did not survive into his composition of the complete play. There one finds of course more than ample evidence of the characters' familiarity with, and implementation of, conventional Irish rural Catholic piety – invocation of the saints, occasional allusion to the Blessed Virgin and, of course, much talk about Father Reilly, the cardinals of Rome and the Pope's dispensation. The social setting of the play is homogeneous as far as Irish denominational difference is concerned – no rector, no peeler of Protestant loyalties, no landlords, agents or bailiffs. Yet the spelling of the Widow Quin's surname, together with the Christian name given for her presumed husband (Marcus Quin), might be thought to suggest a degenerate affiliation to the Protestant Quins [sic] rather than the commonplace Quinns [sic].

Names, as I never tire of saying while tiring many who hear me, say a lot. Pegeen thinks so, when she remarks on Christy's 'quality name' and small feet. Fitzsimon, which featured in an earlier version of this scene, is a name more often found in the plantation county of Cavan than it is in the wilds of Kerry from where the playboy hails. Cavan features in Michael James's drunken song. Closer to the author, one finds his brother Edward Synge in the 1880s and 1890s working as land-agent on the Pratt estate at Cabra Castle, near Kingscourt in County Cavan. The Pratts also had an estate in County Mayo, near Kilalla, just east of the territory invoked in the place-names of *The Playboy*. Edward Synge sometimes worked on this Enniscoe property, especially as an evictor of tenants during the Land War. Migrant workers, displaced farmers, the victims of land-grabbing and broken harvests, emigrants and returned emigrants are alluded to as part of the invisible turbulent society which pushes and shoves outside the door of Michael James Flaherty's respectably licensed public house. Involuntary social mobility characterized Irish history as it runs up, breathless, to the opening moment of this forceful contemporary drama. Some MacBrides of Antrim were moved to Mayo in an effort to engineer a solution to specific conflicts – that's how Major John MacBride is born in Westport in 1865, later to be 'judged to be hanged, quartered and drawn' for treason in 'the ended wars'. Far larger contingents of Orange migrant workers were 'bussed into' Mayo from Ulster to save the hay and reap the harvests of Captain Charles Boycott on Lord Erne's estates where he was agent in 1879-1880. The verb 'to boycott' is nineteenth-century Mayo's best known contribution to the lexicon of English, signifying a refusal to treat with those who break communal codes of solidarity and honour. *The Playboy* could be read as exploring a converse proposition: a communal willingness to absorb (even glorify) those who break the ultimate taboo against patricide.

The most quizzical of the draft elements pertaining to Synge's 1907 masterpiece relate to the play's title. Several were entertained – 'Murder Will Out', 'The Murderer (a Farce)', 'Christy Mahon', 'The Fool of the Family', 'The Fool of Farnham'. Clearly some of these were merely flags of convenience as the author assembled his ideas and developed passages of dialogue: it was sufficient they identified the material for him. 'The Fool of the Family', recently adapted as the title of my biography, continues to give offence – which may have be a calculated risk (or insult) on Synge's part. Nobody – to the best of my knowledge – has discussed the last of the provisional titles as listed above. Clearly 'The Fool of Farnham' parallels 'The Fool of the Family', but the Home Counties town of that denomination seems as remote from Pegeen Mike's kitchen as from the potato field in which the primal deed was essayed. Why Farnham?

Two reasons come to mind. The first reads the title as quasi-autobiographical, just as 'The Fool of the Family' reflected unhappily on the author's relationship with his inheritance. In 1871, Edmund John Millington Synge had been born at Rathfarnham, just south of Dublin city. The place-name was of course an anglicisation of Gaelic elements, unconnected with the South English town. Suffering the various indignities of a genteely impoverished upbringing, and at odds with the ethos of his family, Synge might readily characterize himself in a bitter moment as The Fool of [Rath]Farnham. This portrait of the author as a young Mahon does not seem to me an adequate explanation of the working-title, though it remains relevant.

The second reason depends on a recognition that Farnham is an Irish place-name, though indirectly so. The earl of Farnham held estates in Cavan (including the county town and its jail), and thus introduced his English title to name his Irish seat. In the 1820s, an evangelical movement known as The Second Reformation exacerbated relations between Catholic and Protestant in many parts of Ireland. The Farnham estate in Cavan became a nationally famous refuge for converts and other nervous Protestants during the ensuing clashes and recriminations. Three factors especially render this obscure piece of history relevant to the play we now have as *The Playboy of the Western World*. One is the perception in 1828 that Farnham 'by its local situation was calculated to serve as the conductor of a religious reformation to the Province of Connaught, the peculiar domain of the Roman Catholics'. The second is the use on estates owned by zealots for this Second Reformation of persons known as moral agents, whose role mixed philanthropy and proselytism in a noxious manner: the Farmham estate was one such, the Synge estate at Glanmore in Wicklow was another. The third relates to the ecclesiastical governance of Connaught (or Connacht) effected through the archdiocese of Tuam: among J. M. Synge's direct male ancestors had been the Protestant archbishop of Tuam in the mid-eighteenth century, though the site of a monument erected in his memory was venerated by local Catholics in the late nineteenth century. Pegeen's extraordinary allegation of bestialism, levelled at the Widow Quin, invokes a Lord Bishop of Connaught without preference as to Catholic or Protestant prelate.

The 1820s remain distant from the events alluded to in *The Playboy* – emigration to America, the South African wars, etc. Similarly it may seem that Cavan and Farnham remain unconnected to Michael James Flaherty's licensed public house on the Erris peninsula. Famine and landless 'congestion', the Dublin-focused centralization which railways greatly intensified from the early Victorian period onwards, together with perceptions of loyalist and Protestant Ulster altered with partition from 1920 onwards, all have obscured the social dynamics relating Mayo to other parts of the island. For an illustration of patterns existing in Synge's own life-time, one could do worse than look at the famous boycotting incident of 1880. Charles Cunningham Boycott (1832-1837) was agent on Lord Erne's Mayo estates lying between Lough Mask and Castlebar. When he came into conflict with the Land League, and fell victim to Parnell's policy of sending its enemies to 'moral coventry', Boycott called in assistance from Orange districts in Ulster to save his harvests. In practice, these imported labourers came from counties Monaghan and Cavan. Lists of their names were proudly published in the *Belfast Newsletter* late in 1880, indicating (for the Monaghan men) which estate or townland they hailed from. Though no such detail was provided for the Cavan volunteers, we may be sure that Farnham was not behind the door in defending the old cause for Connacht. The playwright's brother, Edward Synge, arrived on the Pratt estate in Kingscourt while the Boycott expedition was still a topic of lively conversation. It had been a pyrrhic victory of course, for the imported labourers needed a thousand troops for protection.

What better example of a 'broken harvest', that otherwise unattached phrase in Michael James's litany of social disturbance? Little will be served, however, merely by trying to relate the play's background to events on Lord Erne's estate in 1880. A thorough historical reading of *The Playboy of the Western World* requires more than splicing the play's interim title ('Fool of Farnham') with County Cavan's defence of Captain Boycott. The conditions for developing a comprehensive approach are not at the moment entirely propitious. Irish theatre is dominated by so-called cultural tourism. Academic discussion is similarly compromised. The larger arena of cultural debate on the island accommodates so many bill-board warnings about protecting the Good Friday Agreement, and keeping Sinn Féin inside the political process, that inquiries into any historical topic embarrassing to that constituency are not encouraged. But, above all these squalid local considerations, there hangs a cloud of unknowing – the demoralization of historical research itself especially with regard to 'cultural' themes such as theatre or the dangerous intersection of sexuality and politics. As the endless row about Casement's diaries has demonstrated, too much power lies with those twin mutants, the whingeing thug and manipulative toady. These representative types of contemporary Irish intellectual discourse were anticipated by Synge in the characters of Jimmy Farrell and Philly O'Cullen. The recent Peacock Theatre production spotted the incipient Provo in them, drawing on their contribution to a questionnaire based on the traditional complaints of agrarian conspiracy. In the Druid production of February 2004, Garry Hynes presents them as gormless assistant tormentors, visually linked (unconsciously so, perhaps) to the iconography of *Nosferatu, A Symphony of Horror* (1922), FW Murnau's silent film adaptation of Bram Stoker's vampire novel . The pervasive concern is degeneration, whether in its *fin-de-siècle* form (*Dracula*, 1897) or in post-Great-War depression. Synge was placed between these two lurid tableaux of imagery, and a proper historical understanding requires that he should be related both to his past and his future, as well as to the contemporary social reality to which he committed his drama.

The largely erased sub-text of Protestant, biblical allusions, together with incidental Ulster names, scarcely impinges on a stage-performance of *The Playboy of the Western World.* To whatever extent Synge contemplated a play in which sectarian or religio-political difference shaped the encounter of a fugitive with a community, he chose instead to raise no such obstacle to *The Playboy*'s assimilation into a receptive western household. It was suggested in 1907 (or shortly afterwards) that his motives included an element of vengefulness, inspired by the hostile reception given to *In the Shadow of the Glen* and (especially) *The Well of the Saints.* How this may have been, the introduction of an Ulster playboy or a fool of Cavan threatened to exceed the practical capacities of the Irish Edwardian theatre while also reanimating the subjective anxieties which vitiated his first attempt at drama, *When the Moon Has Set*, its author the Fool of Rathfarnham.

Wisely, the mature Synge takes his hero from Kerry and sends him north and westward into Mayo. As Garry Hynes remarked in Galway, no director nowadays differentiates the accents of Christy Mahon and Michael James Flaherty. Yet I have a lingering desire to hear Christy mimic, not voice, his supposed origins, only to have his real identity disclosed by Old Mahon roaring on arrival like Patrick Kavanagh. Or even better, Ian Paisley. Then the faith would be in the fire.

7 | The Playboy of the Western World as Cultural Event

Lionel Pilkington

Peat smoke: that was the audience's first impression of Garry Hynes's 1982 production of *The Playboy of the Western World.* Upon entering Druid Theatre Company's small Chapel Lane auditorium the thick, sweet smell of recently-burnt turf – redolent of rainy days and smoky chimneys in pubs and cottages in Connemara – inaugurated a rambunctious and refreshingly anti-romantic interpretation of Synge's play by a troupe of actors with local accents, visibly dirty hands, and mud-encrusted feet. Reinforced by performances of *The Playboy of the Western World* on the Aran Islands and in other non-traditional rural venues, this early emphasis on authenticity and presence was to become Druid Theatre Company's distinguishing feature. Particularly in the case of Synge (and albeit at a time when postmodernist criticism and theatre practice was attempting to challenge the theatre's traditional reliance on such presence), Hynes's production of *The Playboy of the Western World* conveyed an impression of a theatrical energy that was directly related to the company's own auto-chthonic relationship to the play's West of Ireland location and source. Similar in this respect to Synge's prefatory remarks at the beginning of *The Playboy of the Western World* itself, the Druid Theatre Company achievement was that of re-invigorating Irish theatre in the 1980s by demonstrating the seemingly perennial vitality of a formally and politically conservative theatrical modernism.

If turf smoke prevailed in 1982, it was spotlights in 2004. Approaching Galway's Town Hall Theatre from the street, the opening night audience's first encounter with Hynes's 2004 production of *The Playboy of the Western World* was two roaming spotlights beaming upwards at the night sky. The spotlights were positioned outside the Town Hall's elegant 18th century exterior that was itself draped festively with a huge banner advertising 'DruidSynge'. The banner (a blown up version of the production's poster and programme cover) features a wild-looking man standing in a barrel with one fist held high in the air defiantly clutching a short heavy stick while a similar baton flies past, a few inches above his head. The man's eyes and mouth are wide open and transfixed in an aggressive glare, his lips are blood red, his teeth broken, and his shirt is badly torn. Based on a detail from Jack B. Yeats's 1912 painting 'The Barrel Man', the theatre banner portrayed a fairground activity – the cockshot – that Jack B. Yeats and Synge had witnessed during a visit to Ballina in 1903. For a sum of money thick wooden sticks were purchased and then flung at the dodging head of a man who jumps up from inside a barrel. There is a reference to Christy Mahon's skill in this and other sports at the beginning of Act Three when Philly reports that Christy has broken the nose of the cockshot man. In any case, banner, poster and programme cover offer the audience an arresting image of primitive West of Ireland authenticity.

Once inside the theatre and seated in the auditorium (the smaller Chapel Lane premises is now used almost exclusively for rehearsals), the formal beginning of the production was signalled by a discrete dimming of the house lights and a short pre-performance safety announcement. This announcement was delivered, at least on the night that I attended, in an accent that seemed to have been transplanted directly from the King's Road. We may have been in Galway about to witness a performance of a play about the West of Ireland by a famous Galway-based theatre company, but – the accent suggested –

Poster for the 2004 Druid *Playboy of the Western World*

we need not worry. There would be no embarrassing local solecisms. What we were about to witness – according to all the pre-performance indicators – was a production whose re-presentation of the West of Ireland would be conspicuously mediated: not just by Synge's play, but by the distancing perspectives offered by the Jack B. Yeats's painting on the theatre banner, poster and programme cover, by the Hollywood-style celebrity spotlights outside, and the decidedly metropolitan and non-regional accent of the opening voice-over.

In terms of physical movement and spectacle, Hynes's 2004 production offers a sumptuously rewarding theatrical experience. Its acting, lighting and movement design are all stunningly executed. The light streaming in from the high window on stage right, the empty white light that appears whenever the external door is opened, and the thick ochre red light of the final scene convey an almost operatic impression of a rural community existing in social and geographical isolation, but one whose single visible place of refuge is fraught nevertheless with lurking threat and danger. This was an effect reinforced by Hynes's choice of a Victorian setting. A high-walled, high-windowed and timber-roofed public house is dominated not by a conventional public house bar (as was the custom with earlier productions of *The Playboy of the Western World*) but by a large heavy wooden table shackled to the floor by a metal chain. The table functions as a site for improvisation, games and performance (characters jump on the table, make speeches from it, overturn and hide behind it), while the gaunt chain that tethers it to the floor conveys a troubling, omnipresent and initially puzzling impression of imprisonment. Victorian costumes such as Philly's ill-fitting frock coat and Michael James's stove hat and the caricature-like pairing of the gigantic Philly O'Cullen with the short Jimmy Farrell reinforce the audience's general impression that what is being witnessed is an exaggerated Ireland from another era. Hynes's 2004 production, that is, repudiates realism for a stylish theatricality. It delivers Synge's play from the perspective of a sophisticated metropolitan outsider: at times with the vibrancy of a Jack B. Yeats painting and at times with the Gogolesque satire of a sketch artist for *The Illustrated London News.*

The acting in Hynes's production – particularly that of Cillian Murphy as Christy and Aisling O'Sullivan as the Widow Quin who combine exuberance with moments of isolated solitude – underscores Synge's brilliantly ambivalent treatment of rural Co. Mayo at the beginning of the twentieth century. Just as Synge's play underlines the community's ever-present fictional appetite in terms of the alacrity with which Christy's story of having killed his father is both nourished and accepted and the speed with which Christy is subsequently made into a hero, so Hynes brilliantly exploits every flat surface on stage as a potential place of performance. And just as Christy's story-telling skills and general performativity ('racing, lepping, dancing and the Lord knows what!') result in Christy being lionized as a playboy, so the energy and physical dynamism of the 2004 Druid cast is this production's most memorable and entertaining feature. As for Synge, Hynes's County Mayo community is one for whom performance and improvisation are a vital cultural antidote to boredom, isolation and sexual hunger. All of the play's characters are portrayed as inveterate actors, as suckers for performance. Nevertheless for both the play and the 2004 Druid production, it is this performance and fiction-making addiction that suggests that the only way in which this Co. Mayo community is to be taken seriously is as an object for our entertainment. The culmination of Synge's play is, of course, Pegeen's discovery that there is 'a great gap between a gallous story and a dirty deed', Pegeen's subsequent re-aligning herself with the community and her eschewal of Christy. Discovering that Christy has not, after all, killed his father means that Pegeen realizes that she belongs first of all to the society of the region and, second of all, to herself. She is bound to the community, that is, by its unspoken rule: that the fictionality of a theatrical performance must neither be spelt out nor acknowledged. Paradoxically, then, this is a society that seems incapable of accepting what we as an audience under-stand as theatre. With such flagrant aesthetic myopia in evidence, no wonder that this is a society that is imprisoned. Indeed it is this fundamental point that Hynes's production sets out to underline and develop: the unbridgeable perceptual gap between us, the contemporary theatre audience, and the society represented on stage. Having paid for our tickets and abided by the conventions of theatre spectatorship we know that which the Mayo community seems incapable of knowing: that theatrical performance is always fictional. Of course, there is 'a great gap between a gallous story and a dirty deed': for the theatre spectator that is simply axiomatic. Christy is the only character in the play who understands this rudimentary point, and he finishes the play by walking out on the community with disdain.

Garry Hynes's recent 2004 production develops and accenttuates this feature of Synge's play in an extravagantly theatrical and self-conscious manner. Yet her deliberate widening of the gulf between the perceptual world of the audience and the perceptual world of the characters on the stage is glib and politically very conservative. The characters on stage are, of course, distinctively Irish but they are 'Irish' only in the sense that they are portrayed as socially marginal, materially impoverished and culturally exotic. As with Jack B. Yeats's painting 'The Barrel Man', the theatre audience is transfixed by the spectacle of cultural difference. But unlike, for example, the plays of Suzan Lori Parks or Tony Kushner, there is nothing remotely challenging about Hynes's rendition of this encounter. Instead what separates the theatre audience from the marginalized society on stage is not difference in the sense of incommensurate social and political values, but rather perceptual ability and competence. This rural Irish society – an 'old' Ireland in which the country as a whole was associated with poverty and social, political and economic marginalization – is thus presented as *intrinsically* benighted. Thank goodness, the production seems to say to us, that this Ireland is now so long gone, and how amusing and faint is its memory. In today's multiracial Ireland where the gap between rich and poor is second only to the United States, this is a platitudinous and self-satisfied amnesia. Quintessentially bourgeois, it offers nothing at all in terms of helping us understand the isolating degradations of poverty or of social exclusion. It offers nothing also in assisting us to the related and more difficult understanding: that there are, in fact, varieties of cultural practice and theatrical ex-pression. It is time for Irish theatre to wake up and think again.

8 | Separate Spheres and Celebrity Casting

Paige Reynolds

Before the 2004 Druid Theatre production of Synge's *The Playboy of the Western World*, I had attended only one other staging of the comedy, the 1998 Steppenwolf Theatre production in Chicago, directed by Douglas Hughes. I have pleasant recollections of Steppenwolf's engaging, though fairly traditional, production and particularly of its well calibrated rendering of the play's light humour. But my expectations for the Druid production were not shaped by the wealth of other *Playboys* to which the other conference speakers and attendees liberally referred. While there were many glowing reports of previous versions of the play, including those staged by Druid, some of these accounts suggested to me, perhaps erroneously, that the dominant interpretation of this play merged a Paul Henry painting with a Punch and Judy puppet show. That mixture of furious violence and the familiar iconography of peasant dress and denuded shebeen did not haunt my sense of this play. So while initially uncomfortable with my lack of expertise, I ultimately found it beneficial. Rather than being burdened with the experiences of prior staged interpretations, I had impressions derived almost exclusively from studying, analyzing, and teaching this text. Consequently, my imaginative understanding of *Playboy* has remained quite personal. Of course, every child on the beach thinks her sandcastle is the best, so likely it comes as little surprise that I remain enchanted with my own psychic production. Nonetheless, I found much to appreciate in Druid's rich interpretation of the play. As any good production might, it demanded I rethink the text I thought I knew so well.

The production forcefully exhibited the play's thematic and linguistic contraries, as well as adeptly displaying and heightening the play's necessary tension between humour and horror. The set's nearly windowless public house mirrored the claustrophobia of quotidian life in Mayo, even as the height of its ceiling suggested a kind of freedom from the narrow confines of this greeting place and the fickle community it sheltered. The big visual jokes of this production underscored these oppositions. The drunkenness of the male characters, for instance, registered as both funny and pathetic. Hynes also capitalized effectively on the physical build of her performers. Philly is huge, his friend Jimmy is small; the Widow Quin and Old Mahon are tall, while Pegeen Mike and Christy are diminutive. The size of the performers telegraphed the power dynamics among these relationships. On occasion, this oscillation between contraries failed. I'm thinking here of the excruciatingly slow pace of the opening scene and the rushed tempo, the almost careless careen, of Christy's castigation and exodus. Because of the awkward pacing, the transition in the final act from adoration to repulsion in Pegeen's feelings for Christy felt somewhat false.

Reviews of this production have noted both its realism and its resemblance to the melodrama – observing, in particular, its affinity with the work of the nineteenth-century playwright Dion Boucicault. This tension between realism and melodrama provoked much thought. By reducing psychological complexity in some cases to clear visual cues or broad physical comedy, Hynes was true to the melodramatic impulse in Synge's play. This melodramatic impulse appeared not only in the Victorian costumes and the furniture and accoutrements that littered the set, but also in the response of the twenty-first century audience to this production. Audiences for the historical popular melodrama expected to be entertained by the familiar; they anticipated and were provided elements such as a narrative in which the hero triumphed over the villain and secured the love of the beautiful heroine. Almost a century later, the same anticipation of the familiar and its pleasures similarly characterized this production's audience, who for the most part know what to expect from Synge's renowned comedy.

Hynes's direction worked its magic and many in the audience responded enthusiastically to the bold gestures of her interpretation. Ironically, the production seemed to prey upon the 'easy sentiment' of the popular theatre that the early Abbey worked so hard to challenge with its experimental native drama. Yet even as many members of the audience laughed at the playful account of a primitive community, others clearly suffered through the play's dark and dirty depiction of Irish peasant life early in the previous century. The tension between the production's oppositions – short and tall, melodrama and realism, present and past, humour and pathos – generated a strong production well received by an engaged audience.

The loose brown dirt floor of the shebeen, which shifted with the motions of the characters and sullied their bodies and clothes, provided a realistic touch to the set. But the dirt also offered a device for thinking metaphorically about this production and the notorious history of *The Playboy*. Just as the dirt on the stage floor clung to the hem of each costume, the historical and literary contexts of this play adhered to the production. This Galway performance differed in interesting ways from the *Playboy* offered Dublin audiences nearly a century earlier. For instance, the set for the first *Playboy* was described as unobtrusive, with lime-washed walls and brown fittings that highlighted the bright costumes of the players. In Druid's production, the effect was reversed: the costumes were in muted shades, while the walls were an electric blue. Yet I observed interesting similarities between the two. Both productions provided jaunty performances by a young Widow Quin (performed in 1907 by Sara Allgood and by Aisling O'Sullivan in 2004), and both were offered to a full house of smart, and smartly-dressed, theatre-goers. My favourite moment of synchronicity between past and present fell in the second act of this production. Press accounts of the first production reported that audiences reacted in horror to the gory realism of Old Mahon's gaping, bleeding head wound. Our twenty-first century audience, one accustomed to the graphic violence of television and film, had the identical reaction. I was delighted when the audience loudly 'eewed' at the sight of Old Mahon's bloody, bandaged head.

The production also recalled to me the wonder with which Synge described the separate spheres of men and women in *The Aran Islands*, his ethnographic account of western peasant life in Ireland. In this production, Hynes blocked many scenes so that the worlds of men and women were kept physically separate. As Christy acts out his patricide in act two, he is at a remove from the Mayo girls and the Widow Quin, distanced from them by the large wooden table that commanded the stage. Similarly, in the final act, Christy is pulled from behind by a rope the Mayo men clutch, while Pegeen Mike stands before Christy with a chair strategically placed to distance her from her former sweetheart. More generally, the production seemed to revel in the passions, danger, and humour of *The Aran Islands* – and to demonstrate how drink, recreation, and a good story could recalibrate the dynamics of both the male and female communities.

Those communities provide, I think, what best distinguished this production. I was tremendously impressed by the performances of the supporting cast. As a reader of the comedy, I have always favored the 'small farmers', Jimmy and Philly, and the 'village girls', Sara, Susan, and Honor. They make me laugh – and they provide a mixed chorus of silliness offering rich insight to the world around them, a seemingly incidental commentary that adds invaluable depth both to the love triangle of Christy, Pegeen, and the Widow Quin and to the father-son relationship of Christy and Old Mahon. The performances of the supporting cast made those characters come alive in a way that called attention to the fundamental importance of community in this play.

These supporting characters also added depth to the darker aspects of this production. In act two, Sara Tansey, wonderfully played by Sonya Kelly, enters the shebeen, picks up Christy's boots, and seeks for clues of his violent crime in the 'whity mud, and red mud, and turf...and the fine sands of the sea' stuck to his boots. At that moment, she tries on Christy's boots, which she notes fit her well. On the one hand, Sara's gesture offered us eye candy, and we laughed at the spectacle of this girl loping about in a man's shoes. But on a more profound level it also suggested that Sara is eager 'to walk in Christy's shoes' – that is, she wishes to step into a role that might permit her the opportunities and freedoms that allowed Christy to kill his father, to set out in the wide world, and to escape the burdens of paternity and patriarchy. In this moment, the limits of female power in this world, and the small compensations offered by imagination to the women of Mayo, were highlighted with startling clarity. This production forever transformed a scene I had regarded as strictly playful into one that also allowed for critique.

This comic scene was particularly powerful because it reverberated with the haunting opening scene of the play in which Pegeen – slowly, reluctantly, and almost painfully – orders her trousseau, a trousseau that must be sent not directly to her but to her father, 'Mister Michael James Flaherty' – despite the fact that she orders the goods and, more likely than not, performed the labor that earned the money to pay for them. I was similarly struck in the second act by the struggle between Pegeen Mike and the strong, charismatic Widow Quin. In this scene, Pegeen and Quin command the stage as Christy observes, a turnabout from the opening of the act in which Christy performed for the village girls. The female performances here popped with energy, promise, and desperation. In fact, Christy almost disappeared in this scene, shrinking over his plate as the two women fought – not over the right to him, it almost seemed, but for the rare opportunity to assert dominance. Christy became merely a pretext for their battle, for the tiny bit of authority they could seize and display to each other.

In this scene, Pegeen was somewhat lacklustre, perhaps because Anne-Marie Duff lacked the presence and experience to compete with more seasoned stage actors. But even in that ostensible weakness, we might infer that the Widow Quin, for all the obvious pain and suffering of her life, has a type of autonomy and therefore an allure for contemporary audiences that Pegeen does not. Maligned by the community, the Widow Quin can nonetheless bargain with Shawn Keogh, even if their deal ultimately fails; she can direct Christy's behaviour, even though he repeatedly defies her; she can imagine, if not take on, a life outside Mayo; and she can control, albeit only briefly, the space she inhabits by virtue of the limited freedoms allowed her by widowhood. In the shadow of O'Sullivan's dynamic widow, Duff's Pegeen can be only a daughter, constricted by her attachment to the shebeen, to her father, and to the role ascribed her by society.

Duff's performance did, however, highlight a moment easily overlooked in act one when Pegeen marvels at Christy's defiant behaviour, saying, 'I never cursed my father the like of that, though I'm twenty and more years of age.' Less self-sufficient, this Pegeen is eerily similar to the young women of the village whom she disdains. Likewise, these scenes among the female performers added a new dimension to the comedy's close. When Christy departs after the high voltage struggle between him and the villagers, Michael and his male compatriots rush to right the large, and unwieldy, furniture – as if to assert, despite evidence to the contrary, that their world will return to normal after the intense acts and emotions elicited from the women by Christy's presence.

In the 1998 Steppenwolf Theatre production, the American film and theatre actor Martha Plimpton provided the celebrity appeal. Best known for her roles in Ron Howard's *Parenthood* (1989) and Ted Demme's *Beautiful Girls* (1996), Plimpton was frequently typecast as a defiant teenager, and those extra-theatrical associations drove her Pegeen along a very different vector, as that of a rebellious daughter or wisecracking love interest. In the 2004 Druid production, Pegeen was played by Anne-Marie Duff, whom I associate with her recent powerful performance in Peter Mullan's *The Magdalene Sisters* (2002) as Margaret, the young woman raped and institutionalized. Through her casting choice for Pegeen, Hynes further emphasized the constraints placed on Irish women; but Duff's association with her earlier role as Margaret pulled the play in another direction. Pegeen seemed more brittle, and less playful, than I had imagined the character. My sense of Duff's Pegeen stems locally from her somewhat muted and constrained performance, but my perceptions were likely influenced also by her film role as Margaret.

The other celebrity casting coup of this production – Cillian Murphy performing Christy Mahon – seemed to me more successful. His physical delicacy seemed ideal for the part: he did in fact appear a young man with small feet and a 'noble brow'. Christy is necessarily androgynous, and Murphy splendidly embodied that quality. He didn't command the stage, but surprisingly, in this production that retraction seemed appropriate. Christy is unsure of himself in his new context, before his new audience. Both Murphy and his Christy stand on the cusp of fame; they find themselves awash in a precipitous rush of public enthusiasm, insecure about how their audiences will ultimately regard them.

For any production of *Playboy*, the difficulty seems to be how to drive the play to its final line. That places a tremendous burden on all of the performers, particularly (and obviously) on those actors who play Christy and Pegeen, and who must generate the frisson that explains the anguishing conclusion. The audience should understand, through the ineffable mood generated by a live production, why Pegeen so quickly and radically revokes her attachment to Christy and why she suffers such distress at his departure. This production suggestively, if sometimes unevenly, insinuates that Pegeen's passion and pride interfered with her desire for the freedoms promised her through marriage to the iconoclastic playboy; by attaching herself to him, she can escape her careless father and the simpering Shawn Keogh. In my opinion, Christy and Pegeen failed to convey the expected erotic energy, but this encouraged fresh attention to other facets of the play. Ultimately, the libidinal energy of this production did not reside with Christy and Pegeen, but instead with the Widow Quin and Old Mahon. When in act three the magisterial Widow Quin assumed her place on Old Mahon's lap, I realized that they were the couple whose story I wanted to follow.

Aisling O'Sullivan as the Widow Quin, Frank O'Sullivan as Old Mahon, in Act Three.

Photograph: Keith Pattison.

My critical assessments of the performances notwithstanding, I believe the casting of this production of *The Playboy of the Western World* is its greatest triumph. When I arrived in Galway and discovered that the entire run of the production had already sold out, I was astonished – and delighted. The same strategy of casting film stars that filled theatres for Broadway's *The Producers* or *Chicago* could work wonders for a harder, richer, better play. The erotic appeal of Cillian Murphy eludes me, but many young theatre goers respond to it perfectly. Stateside, the young women in my freshman course, who struggled through Synge's poetry when we studied *Playboy* early in the school year, swooned with delight when I told them who would act as the playboy for this production. If that marquee casting gets new playgoers to the theatre – audience members who will ideally be enchanted not simply by the sight of Murphy's naked torso, but also by the magic of a gorgeous play realized on stage – then I will happily endure titters among the audience, and less sure performances. Because, after all, the beauty of this play, especially in Ireland but also in the United States, is that it will always be restaged, reinterpreted, and available both to the die-hard Synge fans and those seeking an entertaining night out at the theatre.

Index

Contributors

Ophelia Byrne: Formerly Curator, Theatre and Performing Arts Archive, Linen Hall Library, Belfast; author of *Stage in Ulster from the Eighteenth Century* (1997); ed. *State of Play?* (2001), *The Theatre and Cultural Identity in Twentieth Century Ulster*; member, board of directors, Tinderbox Theatre Company, Belfast.

Lelia Doolan: Lecturer in Galway (NUIG and GMIT) in film and journalism. Long association with theatre, film, television as actor and producer/director. Former Artistic Director, Abbey Theatre; former Chairman, Bord Scannán na hÉireann/Irish Film Board. Currently developing documentaries on social political issues. Contributor to various periodicals; member, editorial board *Irish Communications Review.*

Adrian Frazier: Director, MA in Writing, MA in Drama and Theatre Studies, National University of Ireland, Galway. Author of *Behind the Scenes: Yeats, Horniman, and the Struggle for the AbbeyTheatre* (1990) and *George Moore 1852-1933* (2000); editor of 'Irish Theatre', *the irish review* (Autumn 2002). Currently at work on a book entitled *Hollywood Irish: The Migration of Abbey Actors to the American Screen.*

Nicholas Grene: Professor of English Literature at Trinity College, Dublin. Author of *The Politics of Irish Drama* (1995), *Interpreting Synge: Essays from the Synge Summer School 1991-2000* (2000), *Talking about Tom Murphy* (Carysfort Press, 2002), and other books.

John P. Harrington: Dean of the School of Humanities and Social Sciences at Rensselaer Polytechnic Institute near the New York State capital of Albany. Author of *The Irish Beckett* (1991) and *The Irish Play on the New York Stage* (1997) and editor of the Norton Critical Editions anthology *Modern Irish Drama* (1991). Harrington is President of the American Conference for Irish Studies for 2003-2005 and co-editor of the ACIS volume *Politics and Performance in Contemporary Northern Ireland* (1999), published by University of Massachusetts Press.

Garry Hynes: Founded Druid Theatre, Galway 1975 and worked as its Artistic Director from 1975 to 1991 and again from 1995 to date. Garry was Artistic Director of The Abbey Theatre, Dublin from 1991 to 1994. Druid: Productions include: *Wood of the Whispering, The Shaughraun, The Factory Girls, The Loves of Cass Maguire, The Playboy of the Western World, Bailegangaire, Conversations on a Homecoming, Lovers' Meeting, The Leenane Trilogy* (Royal Court co-production), *On Raftery's Hill* (Royal Court co-production), *The Good Father, Sive, Sharon's Grave.* Abbey Theatre: *Big Maggie, King of the Castle, The Plough and the Stars, The Power of Darkness, Famine, A Whistle in the Dark* (also Royal Court). Other productions include: *Portia Coughlan* (also Royal Court), *The Man of Mode, Song of the Nightingale* (RSC), *The Colleen Bawn* (Royal Exchange, Manchester), *Juno and the Paycock* (Gaiety Theatre), *Mr. Peter's Connections* (Signature Theatre, New York), *Crimes of the Heart* (Second Stage Theatre, New York). *My Brilliant Divorce* (West End), *Crestfall* (Gate, Dublin). Awards: Garry Hynes has been awarded Honorary Doctorates from the National University of Ireland (1998) and the National Council for Education Awards (1988) for her services to Irish Theatre. In 1998 she became the first woman to win a Tony award for Direction for *The Beauty Queen of Leenane.* She received the Irish Times/ESB award last year for Best Director for her production of *Sive* and *The Good Father.*

Mary C. King: Visiting Professor in Cultural Studies at the National College of Ireland. Author of recent articles on Synge, Wilde, Joyce, Marina Carr, Edward Martyn and Martin McDonagh, and of the chapter entitled 'J.M. Synge 'national drama' and the post-Protestant imagination' in *The Cambridge Companion to Irish Theatre* (2004). At present working on Joyce's *Exiles* and the Tulira plays of Edward Martyn.

Bill (W.J.)McCormack: Author of two studies of J.M. Synge and his family background: *Fool of the Family; a Life of JM Synge* (2002), and *The Silence of Barbara Synge* (2003). His political biography of W. B. Yeats, *Blood Kindred*, will be published by Pimlico in spring 2005.

Lionel Pilkington: Lectures in the English Department, NUI, Galway, where he is course director of the MA in Cutlure and Colonialism. Author of *Theatre and State in Twentieth Century Ireland* (2001) and many articles on Irish theatre and cultural politics.

Paige Reynolds: Assistant Professor of English at the College of the Holy Cross in Worcester, Massachusetts. Author of articles in *Twentieth Century Literature, Modernism/Modernity, New Hibernia Review*, and *Irish University Review*, and is currently at work on a monograph tentatively entitled, *'A New Public, A New Form of Life': The Audiences for Irish Modernism.*

CARYSFORT PRESS

The Press aims to produce high quality publications which, though written and/or edited by academics, will be made accessible to a general readership. The organisation would also like to provide a forum for critical thinking in the Arts in Ireland, again keeping the needs and interests of the general public in view.

Carysfort Press was formed in the summer of 1998. It receives annual funding from the Arts Council.

The directors believe that drama is playing an ever-increasing role in today's society and that enjoyment of the theatre, both professional and amateur, currently plays a central part in Irish culture.

The company publishes contemporary Irish writing for and about the theatre.

Editorial and publishing inquiries to:

CARYSFORT PRESS
58 Woodfield, Scholarstown Road,
Rathfarnham, Dublin 16,
Republic of Ireland
T (353 1) 493 7383 F (353 1) 406 9815
e: info@carysfortpress.com
www.carysfortpress.com

NEW TITLES

GOETHE AND SCHUBERT
ACROSS THE DIVIDE

Proceedings of the International Conference, 'Goethe and Schubert in Perspective and Performance', Trinity College Dublin, 2003. This volume includes essays by leading scholars – Barkhoff, Boyle, Byrne, Canisius, Dürr, Fischer, Hill, Kramer, Lamport, Lund, Meikle, Newbould, Norman McKay, White, Whitton, Wright, Youens – on Goethe's musicality and his relationship to Schubert; Schubert's contribution to sacred music and the Lied and his setting of Goethe's Singspiel, Claudine. A companion volume of this Singspiel (with piano reduction and English translation) is also available.

ISBN 1-904505-04-X
Goethe and Schubert:
Across the Divide. €25

ISBN 0-9544290-0-1
Goethe and Schubert:
'Claudine von Villa Bella'. €14

CRITICAL MOMENTS
FINTAN O'TOOLE ON MODERN IRISH THEATRE

This new book on the work of Fintan O'Toole, the internationally acclaimed theatre critic and cultural commentator, offers percussive analyses and assessments of the major plays and playwrights in the canon of modern Irish theatre. Fearless and provocative in his judgements, O'Toole is essential reading for anyone interested in criticism or in the current state of Irish theatre.

ISBN 1-904505-03-1
€20

GEORG BÜCHNER: WOYZECK

A NEW TRANSLATION
BY DAN FARRELLY

The most up-to-date German scholarship of Thomas Michael Mayer and Burghard Dedner has finally made it possible to establish an authentic sequence of scenes. The wide-spread view that this play is a prime example of loose, open theatre is no longer sustainable. Directors and teachers are challenged to "read it again".

ISBN 1-904505-02-3
€10

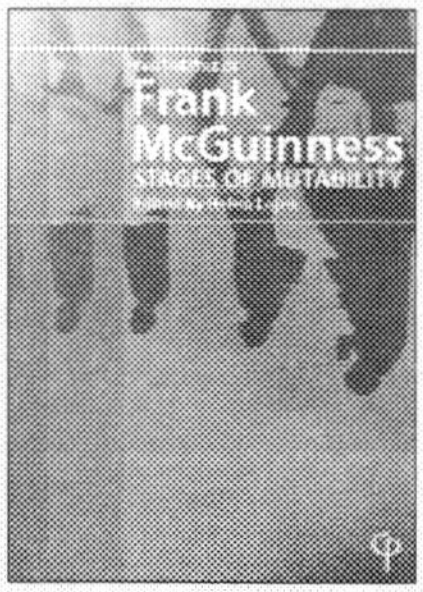

THE THEATRE OF FRANK MCGUINNESS

STAGES OF MUTABILITY
BY HELEN LOJEK

The first edited collection of essays about internationally renowned Irish playwright Frank McGuinness focuses on both performance and text. Interpreters come to diverse conclusions, creating a vigorous dialogue that enriches understanding and reflects a strong consensus about the value of McGuinness's complex work.

ISBN 1-904505-01-5
€15

HAMLET

THE SHAKESPEAREAN DIRECTOR
BY MIKE WILCOCK

"This study of the Shakespearean director as viewed through various interpretations of HAMLET is a welcome addition to our understanding of how essential it is for a director to have a clear vision of a great play. It is an important study from which all of us who love Shakespeare and who understand the importance of continuing contemporary exploration may gain new insights."

From the Foreword, by Joe Dowling, Artistic Director, The Guthrie Theater, Minneapolis, MN

ISBN 1-904505-00-7
€18

THEATRE OF SOUND

RADIO AND THE
DRAMATIC IMAGINATION
BY DERMOT RATTIGAN

An innovative study of the challenges that radio drama poses to the creative imagination of the writer, the production team, and the listener.

"A remarkably fine study of radio drama – everywhere informed by the writer's professional experience of such drama in the making...A new theoretical and analytical approach – informative, illuminating and at all times readable."

Richard Allen Cave

ISBN 0-9534-2575-4
€20

NEW TITLES

THE THEATRE OF MARINA CARR

"BEFORE RULES WAS MADE"
EDITED BY ANNA MCMULLAN
& CATHY LEENEY

As the first published collection of articles on the theatre of Marina Carr, this volume explores the world of Carr's theatrical imagination, the place of her plays in comtemporary theatre in Ireland and abroad and the significance of her highly individual voice.

ISBN 0-9534-2577-0
€20

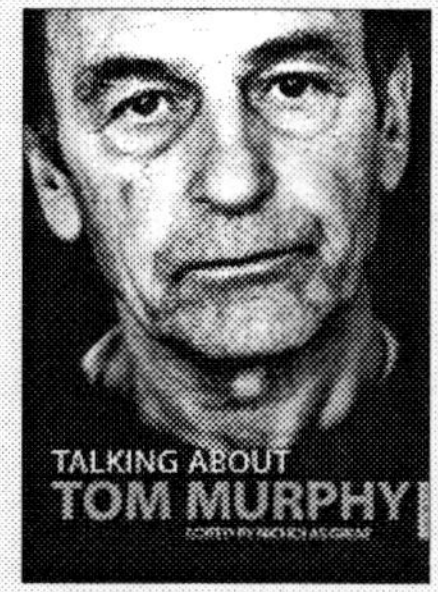

TALKING ABOUT TOM MURPHY

EDITED BY NICHOLAS GRENE

Talking About Tom Murphy is shaped around the six plays in the landmark Abbey Theatre Murphy Season of 2001, assembling some of the best-known commentators on his work: Fintan O'Toole, Chris Morash, Lionel Pilkington, Alexandra Poulain, Shaun Richards, Nicholas Grene and Declan Kiberd.

ISBN 0-9534-2579-7
€10

BACK LIST

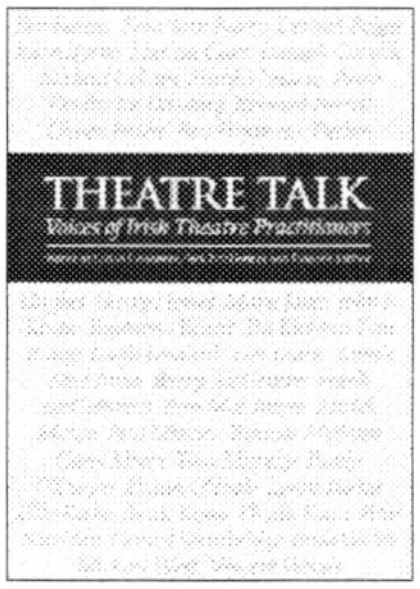

THEATRE TALK

VOICES OF IRISH THEATRE PRACTITIONERS
EDITED BY LILIAN CHAMBERS, GER FITZGIBBON & EAMONN JORDAN

"This book is the right approach - asking practitioners what they feel."

Sebastian Barry, Playwright.

"... an invaluable and informative collection of interviews with those who make and shape the landscape of Irish Theatre."

Ben Barnes, Artistic Director of the Abbey Theatre

ISBN 0-9534-2576-2
€20

IN SEARCH OF THE SOUTH AFRICAN IPHIGENIE

BY ERIKA VON WIETERSHEIM
AND DAN FARRELLY

Discussions of Goethe's "Iphigenie auf Tauris" (Under the Curse) as relevant to women's issues in modern South Africa: women in family and public life; the force of women's spirituality; experience of personal relationships; attitudes to parents and ancestors; involvement with religion.

ISBN 0-9534-2578-9
€10

THE STARVING AND OCTOBER SONG

TWO CONTEMPORARY IRISH PLAYS
BY ANDREW HINDS

The Starving, set during and after the siege of Derry in 1689, is a moving and engrossing drama of the emotional journey of two men.

October Song, a superbly written family drama set in real time in pre-ceasefire Derry.

ISBN 0-9534-2574-6
€10

SEEN AND HEARD (REPRINT)

SIX NEW PLAYS BY IRISH WOMEN
EDITED WITH AN INTRODUCTION BY CATHY LEENEY

A rich and funny, moving and theatrically exciting collection of plays by Mary Elizabeth Burke-Kennedy, Síofra Campbell, Emma Donoghue, Anne Le Marquand Hartigan, Michelle Read and Dolores Walshe.

ISBN 0-9534-2573-8
€20

UNDER THE CURSE

GOETHE'S "IPHIGENIE AUF TAURIS", IN A NEW VERSION
BY DAN FARRELLY

The Greek myth of Iphigenie grappling with the curse on the house of Atreus is brought vividly to life. This version is currently being used in Johannesburg to explore problems of ancestry, religion, and Black African women's spirituality.

ISBN 0-9534-2572-X
€8.25

URFAUST

A NEW VERSION OF GOETHE'S EARLY "FAUST" IN BRECHTIAN MODE
BY DAN FARRELLY

This version is based on Brecht's irreverent and daring re-interpretation of the German classic.

"Urfaust is a kind of well-spring for German theatre… The love-story is the most daring and the most profound in German dramatic literature." *Brecht*

ISBN 0-9534257-0-3
€7.60

THEATRE STUFF (REPRINT)

CRITICAL ESSAYS ON CONTEMPORARY IRISH THEATRE

EDITED BY EAMONN JORDAN

Best selling essays on the successes and debates of contemporary Irish theatre at home and abroad.

Contributors include: Thomas Kilroy, Declan Hughes, Anna McMullan, Declan Kiberd, Deirdre Mulrooney, Fintan O'Toole, Christopher Murray, Caoimhe McAvinchey and Terry Eagleton.

ISBN 0-9534-2571-1
€19

HOW TO ORDER

TRADE ORDERS DIRECTLY TO

CMD
Columba Mercier Distribution
55A Spruce Avenue
Stillorgan Industrial Park
Blackrock
Co. Dublin

T (353 1) 294 2560
F (353 1) 294 2564
E cmd@columba.ie

or contact

SALES@BROOKSIDE.IE